Kindle Formatting

The <u>Complete</u> Guide to Formatting
Books for the Amazon Kindle

by

Joshua Tallent

eBookArchitects.com
KindleFormatting.com

For Lindsey

Contents

Index of Kindle Secrets

Some unique info in this book you won't find anywhere else

Preface

I started thinking about writing this book in late 2007 when I first began working with Kindle eBooks. I saw how so many authors and publishers were spinning their wheels trying publish their books on the Kindle, without knowing how to make that happen easily, if at all. As I started working more with the Kindle and figuring out its quirks, I began to realize that this book was desperately needed.

As with every book, this one was made possible as a result of the support and encouragement I have received from the wonderful people around me.

I would first like to thank my wife, Lindsey, for her unflagging support of me and of my work. Sweetheart, I would not be the man I am now without your love. Thank you for believing in me and supporting me.

My two sweet little girls deserve a ton of love and kisses. Thank you both for understanding the times when Abba had to work instead of play and for decorating my walls with beautiful reminders of your love.

Many thanks also go to my amazing friends, who have not only put up with my incessant talk about formatting Kindle books and my formatting business, but have also stepped in to help in so many ways.

Toby, I am constantly blessed by your friendship; thank you for your willingness to listen and to actually do some coding—and for helping me relax with video games. Wooloolooo!

Israel, your work on the formatting processes has been a great source of joy and relief to me, and your friendship is beyond measure.

Derek, your willing ear and balanced perspectives are of greater value to me than you might think. Thank you for being the friend that sets me straight and ensures that I am not jumping the gun.

I would also like to thank my brother, Richard, for his help testing the Kindle screen's image abilities. He was able to easily figure out important information that had eluded me and many others for months.

Todd Hargis, a photographer here in Austin, took the beautiful photographs on the front cover and in the interior of this book. His flexibility and expertise were instrumental in the final product looking as great as it does. Please visit his website at www.pbase.com/todd991.

Lastly, I am grateful to my many KindleFormatting.com clients. Your willingness to support my work and give me access your own is how this book came into existence.

Joshua Tallent
Austin, Texas
March 2009

Introduction

Electronic books (eBooks) are the future of books and book reading. While I am convinced that paper books will never entirely disappear, the introduction of eBooks into the mass market is, in my opinion, an event on the same scale as the invention of the moveable type printing press.

At the center of the eBook revolution are the various eBook reading devices on the market today, and one of the most popular of those eBook devices is the Amazon Kindle. The Kindle is the first eBook reader to allow completely wireless purchasing and downloading of books without the need to use a computer. This innovation, coupled with the large and expanding number of books that Amazon has made available to Kindle owners, has fueled an intense change in perspective regarding the value and future of eBooks.

Amazon made another key decision with the creation of the Kindle. The company opened up the door for anyone to publish content via the Digital Text Platform (DTP). Independent authors and small publishers instantly had the ability to compete in a substantial portion of the eBook market with the big publishing houses, and they have jumped at that opportunity. The number of titles available in the Kindle store has grown steadily since the store first opened for business, doubling in the first year. Fiction and non-fiction, short and long, big publishers and first-time authors—all have a role in the eBook industry.

The problem is that most people don't know how to create a well-formatted Kindle eBook. From the beginning, the DTP user forums were full of questions about how to get the formatting to look good, or how to fix a specific problem that just doesn't seem to go away.

That is why I have written this book. As a professional eBook developer and the first eBook developer to offer Kindle-specific formatting services I have seen many authors and publishers struggle with the formatting in their books, never knowing exactly how to get the book to look right on the Kindle screen. This struggle is not without reason. The foundational Kindle file format is a stripped down version of HTML, the programming language used to create websites. Most authors and publishers are not familiar with HTML, and the Kindle's specific implementation of it is not generally intuitive.

The Kindle format is actually the same format that is used in Mobipocket eBooks. Amazon purchased Mobipocket in March 2005, allowing the company to use a widely accepted format and import a large number of books for sale on the Kindle from the start. This has contributed greatly to the Kindle's success, and it provides even better opportunities for authors and publishers to make their books available to a wide audience through the Mobipocket eBookBase.

Kindle 2 and Kindle on the iPhone

In February 2009, Amazon released an updated version of the Kindle eBook reader. The "Kindle 2" sports a more streamlined look and few nice tweaks under the hood. The formatting differences between the two devices will be discussed below.

In March 2009, Amazon released an iPhone application that allows Kindle users to read their eBooks on the iPhone, as well. The eBooks in the new app are similar in appearance to the Kindle, and the basic formatting described in this book will work fine in the app.

About this book

This is not a guide to marketing your book for the Kindle or Mobipocket; there are other more experienced publishers and self-publishing gurus who can assist you in that part of your process. The purpose of this book is to provide you with an easy-to-follow guide to converting your books into the Kindle format. In addition, this book is intended to be a resource for anyone who needs to know what HTML the Kindle supports, how to format problematic and special types of text, and other more advanced issues related to Kindle eBook formatting.

The chapters below cover how to get your book into a usable file type, how to clean up the code so that it is easier to format, and how to add formatting directly to the HTML code to see the best results in your final Kindle book. That is actually the most useful information in this book. In Chapters 5 and 6, I give detailed descriptions and examples of the formatting you can use on the Kindle, including some unique approaches to making the formatting match a print book. Then, Chapter 7 shows you how to make a Mobipocket book, which allows for some great little features in the Kindle 2.

Each section is written with the intention of being somewhat self-contained. You can use this book for reference only, or read it straight through and follow each step as you format your book. However, be sure to read a section entirely before doing anything, since I might give more information or alternate approaches further down the page.

Of course, there are always questions and issues that arise in the process of converting a print book into an eBook. If you need assistance, please feel free to visit my website or drop me a line at joshua@kindleformatting.com.

In addition to the resources in this book, I have created a set of downloadable files on my website, all of which will help you format your Kindle book. You can access those files at:

http://kindleformatting.com/book

I am also available to help you with a wide variety of eBook-related services. See a description of those services on page 137 or at my website.

Chapter 1

Getting Your Content into a Useable Format

The first step in creating a well-formatted Kindle book is to get your content into a file format you can use. Because Kindle books are all HTML behind the scenes, HTML is the best format to start and finish with. However, HTML editing and formatting can require a significant learning curve, especially if you are dealing with content that has a lot of specific formatting and layout requirements.

With that in mind, I will show you in Chapters 2 and 3 how to convert your book into a clean HTML file both by cleaning it up in Microsoft Word and by handling the HTML directly. To that end, the first step in your conversion process is to decide which of these two routes you will take. Then you will determine the best way to get the contents of your book into the chosen format.

Microsoft Word (a word processing program that is part of the Microsoft Office suite) is a well-known tool that is installed on millions of computers worldwide. There are other word processing programs available, such as Open Office and WordPerfect, and many of the instructions in Chapter 2 will apply to the output of those programs as well. However, due to the popularity of Word and the fact that it generates relatively clean and consistent HTML when used properly, the instructions below will be geared toward its use.

HTML is a programming language that creates visual formatting by the addition of "tags" around the text of the file. For instance, to make some text bold in HTML you would add ... tags around the text, like this:

```
<b>some bolded text here</b>
```

Which format you decide to use to cleanup your book is completely up to you. Word is easier for someone who is not familiar with HTML or coding in general, but HTML is usually faster to work with and more precise. Just remember that because the Kindle's format is HTML-based, you will be making at least a few adjustments to your book in HTML regardless of whether you start with it or not.

Current Format

The file format your book is in right now will be a determining factor in how you decide to proceed. Some authors only have access to the final PDF file their publisher sent them after the book was laid out and formatted for publication. Other authors may be starting with a Word document, never having had their book published. Sometimes all an author has available is a plain text document with no formatting, and other times, especially with out-of-print books, they only have a hardcopy. Publishers, on the other hand, often have the InDesign or Quark files used in preparing the book for publication. Each of these formats has the potential to be either a great help or a hindrance to the development of your eBook.

Let's walk through the process of converting books in these various formats into HTML or Word, discussing the pros and cons of the conversion options available.

InDesign

Adobe's InDesign software is quickly becoming the book layout product of choice by publishers everywhere. It is versatile and feature-rich, and has the ability to make a designer's work much easier to do. It also includes a new feature that was not present in earlier editions of InDesign: Export to XHTML. What's this? Another acronym? XHTML is

HTML with additional rules applied to make it cleaner. Those rules end up being a great benefit if you decide to export the text this way.

The Cross-media Export option in InDesign CS3 gives you three options: XML, XHTML/Dreamweaver, and XHTML/Digital Editions. The XML export is likely to be completely useless since most designers do not build their books with XML tagging. The XHTML/Digital Editions option will create an ePub file, from which you can extract useable XHTML files. To do that, save the .epub file to your computer, change the extension to ".zip", and open the file with your computer's zip utility. In the OEBPS folder you will find a selection of XHTML files, as well as a CSS file. Extract these to a folder of your choosing and get to work. At some point, whether now or later, you will want to combine all of those XHTML files together into one big file, with the content in the right order. That order can be seen in the toc.ncx file, which appears in the OEBPS folder and which you can open in your text editor like an XHTML file.

You can also use the XHTML/Dreamweaver option. The name is misleading since you do not actually need Adobe's Dreamweaver program to edit the output file, but the XHTML should be fairly clean despite that fact.

After you export the book with either XHTML option you will want to look at the code (see Chapter 3) to make sure that you still have all of your basic formatting like bold and italics, that all of your text is still present, and that your book is not messed up in any other way. If it is, you might have some luck changing the formatting of the InDesign file before attempting to export the book again, but you may also have to add in the missing content or styles by hand.

QuarkXPress

QuarkXPress is another book layout program that is used by some publishers. The latest version of the software has an HTML export feature, but, as with InDesign, your mileage may vary. To use the export feature, open the QuarkXPress file and duplicate the layout through Layout, Duplicate. While duplicating, set the Medium Type as Web in the

Duplicate Layout dialog. This web layout can then be exported as HTML from File, Export. The program will probably save each page of your book as individual HTML files, so you will need to find a way to combine them together. (I have a sample Perl script in the book downloads section of my website.) Also, be sure to look at the exported HTML file and ensure that you did not lose any major formatting in the process.

PDF

Adobe's PDF format is the most common file type that authors and publishers have available to them. There are a variety of options available to authors for getting a PDF file into useable HTML. The HTML resulting from these conversion processes will vary greatly. Some will provide you with really sparse code that does not contain all of the original formatting. Others will provide you with all of your formatting, but code that is bloated and messy. I suggest you try all of these options and look at the various outputs you get before deciding which one to go with.

Adobe Online Conversion. Adobe has a free online conversion tool intended for the vision-impaired that will convert a PDF file into HTML. You can use this free tool by emailing the file to pdf2html@adobe.com. Adobe also offers a PDF to text conversion using the e-mail address pdf2txt@adobe.com. Both of these services will respond to your e-mail with an attachment of the files you sent converted into HTML.

Third-party conversion tools. Other companies have produced PDF-to-HTML conversion software programs. A simple search on any Web search engine will provide you with a list of options. Some programs are as inexpensive as $50.00, and other programs may be free. While all of these programs will export HTML from your PDF, the quality of the HTML and how much work will be required to clean it up will vary based on the quality of the program. Most of the programs available will provide you with the option of downloading a trial version which you can use for a limited amount of time. These trial versions are usually fully functional and you should be able to convert your book without any problems. If you find that the conversion looks great and is usable, you should consider purchasing the program.

Mobipocket Creator. Another option for getting a PDF file into HTML is to use Mobipocket Creator. Since the Kindle uses the Mobipocket eBook format, the HTML that results from a Mobipocket Creator conversion is supposed to be at least a little bit closer to what you want in the final file. This is sometimes the case, and I must say that Mobipocket does a great job of reducing the amount of extraneous code and formatting you see in most other conversion processes. The main drawback is that it occasionally loses or discards some of the formatting you may want it to keep. Also, it is currently only available for Windows computers, so Mac and Linux users may be out of luck. That being said, I heartily endorse Mobipocket Creator for the majority of PDF to HTML conversion jobs.

Follow these steps to import your file to Mobipocket Creator and find the resulting HTML:

1. Download Mobipocket Creator from: http://www.mobipocket.com/en/downloadSoft/ProductDetailsCreator.asp

2. Install the software on your Windows computer.

3. Open Creator. You will by default see the "Home" page.

4. Drag and drop your PDF file onto the Creator window. Alternatively, you can click on "Import from Existing File, Adobe PDF", then click the Browse button and find your PDF file that way.

5. Click Import.

6. Open your "My Publications" directory, which is usually placed in your "My Documents" directory by default. In the "My Publications" directory you will find another directory with the same name as the PDF file you uploaded ("My Publications/*MyBook*"). Open that directory.

7. Inside you will see an HTML file, any images included in the book, the original PDF file, and two or three other files that are not relevant to the current discussion (XML, OPF, PRC). You can leave the HTML and image files there or move them somewhere else for formatting.

Convert to Word. I have found that converting a PDF into HTML is much easier when you first convert it into the Microsoft Word format. This is even true of PDF files converted using Adobe Acrobat. While Microsoft Word does not do a perfect job of converting its documents into HTML, the number of HTML tags that are created by Word is usually much lower than the number of tags created directly by Acrobat (see an example of this in Chapter 4). With that in mind there are also tools available online that will convert a PDF file into a Microsoft Word document. Again, the quality of the resulting file will vary based on the quality of the tool.

Adobe Acrobat Professional. If you have a copy of Adobe Acrobat, or if you have downloaded the trial version, I suggest that you export your PDF as a Word document first and follow the instructions below to convert that Word document into HTML. That is the process that I use for most of the PDF books that come to me in my Kindle formatting business. To export the file, simply go to the File menu in Acrobat, select the Export option, and choose the Word document option from the dropdown menu. You can also use the Save As feature with the same results.

If your book is very large or has a large number of images, you may find that Acrobat will stop responding during the conversion. The best way to remedy this problem is to split your file into smaller pieces and convert each piece separately.

- Go to the Document menu.
- Select Extract Pages.
- In the dialog box, choose the pages you want to extract.
- Those pages will be pulled into a new PDF file that you will need to save and convert as explained above.

Word and RTF

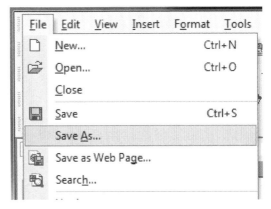

Whether you have written your book in Microsoft Word or have converted it from another format, the process of creating HTML from the Word document is fairly simple. This conversion process only works natively on Word 2002/XP and later, but there is a plug-in available for Word 2000. Go to the File menu (in Word 2007, click the Office Button) and select the Save As option. In the Save As dialog box, click on the dropdown next to "Save as Type." From that list, choose "Web Page, Filtered." You will be given a couple of warning messages, but they are usually not a problem.

If your file is large or has lots of images, Word may lock up during the save and become unresponsive. If this happens, you should split the file into pieces and save each one as HTML individually. The easiest way to do this is to cut and paste sections of the book into new Word documents.

If you have an RTF or WordPerfect document you can open it in Word and follow these same steps to get the file into HTML. WordPerfect also has a "Publish To" feature that allows you to save the file as HTML, and you may find that that feature works best for your book.

Of course, you may want to do some cleanup on the Word file before you save it as HTML. If that is the case, follow the instructions in Chapter 2 first.

Note that you can also import the Word document into Mobipocket Creator and let it convert the file into HTML. The resulting code will be much less bloated than what you get in the Save as HTML function, but it may also be missing some formatting you needed. If you use this process, be sure to look carefully through your file to ensure your formatting is still in place.

Follow these steps to import your file and find the resulting HTML:

1. Download Mobipocket Creator from: http://www.mobipocket.com/en/downloadSoft/ProductDetailsCreator.asp

2. Install the software on your Windows computer.

3. Open Creator. You will by default see the "Home" page.

4. Drag and drop your Word file onto the Creator Window. Alternatively, you can click on "Import from Existing File, MS Word document", then click the Browse button and find your Word file that way.

5. Click Import.

6. Open your "My Publications" directory, which can usually be found in your "My Documents" directory by default. In the "My Publications" directory you will find another directory with the same name as the Word file you uploaded ("My Publications/*MyBook*"). Open that directory.

7. Inside you will see an HTML file, any images included in the book, the original Word file, and two or three other files that are not relevant to the current discussion (XML, OPF, PRC). You can leave the HTML and image files there or move them somewhere else for formatting.

Text Documents

If your file is in a text-only format (i.e., with no formatting), it is not too difficult to prepare it for publication in the Kindle. You can add the HTML mark-up yourself (see Chapter 5) or paste the text into a Word document and following the formatting procedures listed in Chapter 2.

HTML and XML

If your document is already in HTML or XML, especially if the code is relatively clean, you are already a long way toward the goal of getting your book into the Kindle format. You can move on to Chapter 3 and start your process there.

No Digital File

There are times when an author or publisher only has a physical copy of the book they want to publish on the Kindle. This is most common with out-of-print books, but it can also happen when the rights to the book revert back to the author and the publisher, for whatever reason, does not have a copy of the book in a PDF or other digital format. The easiest way to get the book back into a digital format is to scan it and run it through an Optical Character Recognition (OCR) software program.

There are a variety of options available to the do-it-yourself person or to the pay-someone-else person. The main benefit to doing the process yourself is saving money, but you may find that having some help in the process is easier and faster.

The first step in the OCR process is to have your book scanned. This is a process where each page of your book is turned into an image that can be loaded into the OCR program. There are a variety of places that will do scanning for you, or you can tackle the process yourself. Some copy and print stores (like FedEx/Kinko's) offer scanning services, but you will often find the best prices at companies that specialize in scanning documents onto microfiche. Some of these companies even have machines that can automate the scanning process by automatically turning the pages of the book.

Be aware that the easiest way to scan a book is to cut off the binding, which will effectively ruin the book. If your book is rare and you want to keep it intact, you should make sure the scanning company knows to handle it gently and to not cut off the binding.

If you decide to scan the book yourself, you will need a flatbed or feed scanner. These devices are available at most electronics and computer stores and at various retailers online. They can be inexpensive or very expensive, depending on the options included and the quality of the scanner, and you may find that the available options are overwhelming. In general, any low-end scanner will do the job, but you may want to ensure that it comes with a built-in OCR program (more on that in a moment). Flatbed scanners will require you to position each page, while feed scanners make the process a bit faster by pulling the pages in one at a time like a copier. Realize, though, that if you are only going to scan one book you will spend almost as much money on the scanner as you will sending the book to a professional scanning company.

The next step in the OCR process is running the page images through an OCR software program. If you are not interested in handling the OCR process yourself, there are many companies out there that can do the OCR work for you. In addition to searching for these companies online, you should ask the company that scans your book if they can suggest someone to do the OCR process. They may even offer those services in-house.

If you are scanning the book yourself, your scanner may be installed with an option to OCR the text of the scanned pages and save them in Microsoft Word or another format. Many times the software used by these scanners is a "lite" version of ABBYY FineReader, which is, in my opinion, the best OCR software on the market. The scanned text will undoubtedly have some errors, but you may find that scanning at a higher DPI or adding more contrast to the images affects the OCR results significantly. Just remember to keep your Word files named in ,a consistent order so that you are easily able to add them together and edit them later.

If you are converting a large number of books using an OCR process, you should consider investing in an OCR software program. I have used a variety of OCR programs over the years, and I cannot suggest any program except ABBYY FineReader for large-scale processes. ABBYY has a built-in document viewer, which allows you to easily make changes to the OCR output and fix the errors that ABBYY is not sure about. It also exports the output to a variety of formats, including HTML and Word.

Chapter 2

Formatting your book in Microsoft Word

Most authors are not familiar with HTML code and are not in a position to learn it just for the purpose of preparing their book for the Kindle. The fact is, you can easily format a simple Kindle book in Microsoft Word without the need to work with the HTML very much unless you really want to. The key to this formatting process is mastering the use of Word's built-in Styles and understanding how certain formatting will look on the Kindle itself.

The instructions and comments below are based on the assumption that you have your book text in a Word document. If you have converted it into HTML, you can skip to Chapter 3 to learn how to work with the HTML code. However, if you like, you can also open your HTML file in Word and save it as a .doc file, then follow the instructions below.

Word's Styles and Formatting Options

Microsoft Word has a Styles feature that allows you to easily format a document in a very consistent way. When you apply styles to the headings, paragraphs, and other items in your book, you can then make changes to those items all in one place. The changes made will automatically be applied to every item formatted in that style, cutting down drastically on the amount of work needed to make sweeping changes to your book.

Another benefit to using Styles is that the foundational code ends up being much cleaner. If you decide to do some manual HTML cleanup before publishing, the styles you used in Word will be easy to change in the HTML file. Also, if you decide to upload the Word doc itself to Amazon's Digital Text Platform (DTP), the chances of seeing major formatting issues after the Kindle conversion decrease dramatically.

Understanding Styles

When you first create a new Word document it is assigned a small set of default styles. However, if you are working with a book that was saved from another format or that was styled in Word without using the built-in Styles feature, the list of styles can be fairly long. Essentially, every paragraph that has a unique format, every heading with a slight variation, and every phrase that has its own special formatting will have its own style listed. Your goal in this process is to pare down your list to the most essential styles so that you have fewer variables to deal with.

To get started, you will need to open the Styles and Formatting sidebar in Word. In older editions of Word, select the Format menu at the top of the window and choose "Styles and Formatting..." from the dropdown list (Figure 2.1). You will now see the sidebar on the right side of the Word window, complete with a list of the styles that are being used or are available for document (Figure 2.2).

In Word 2007, the interface is a little bit different. The Styles are shown in the Home tab (Figure 2.3), and you can click on the dropdown arrow to see the full list of available styles (Figure 2.4). To open the Styles sidebar, click on the pop-out arrow under the "Change Styles" button (Figure 2.5). The sidebar is a floating, always-on-top window that you can position anywhere on your screen (Figure 2.6).

You should take a few minutes to familiarize yourself with the sidebar. Notice that if you click the dropdown arrow next to a style or right-click on the style name you will be given some options, including one to select all of the places in the document that use that style. This can be useful as

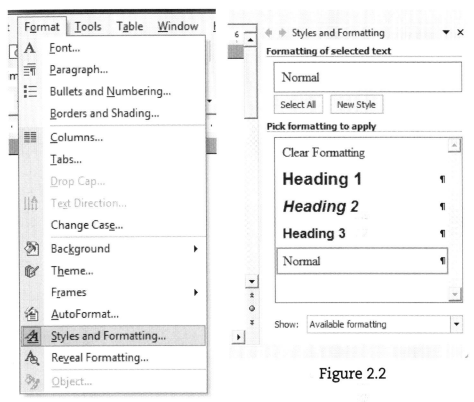

Figure 2.1

Figure 2.2

Figure 2.3

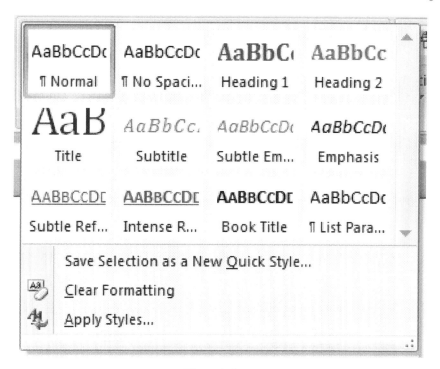

Figure 2.4

Figure 2.5

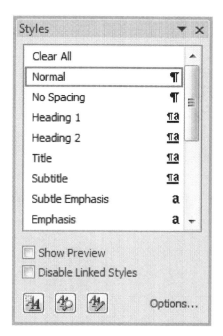

Figure 2.6

you consolidate styles and make the formatting more consistent. You will also see an option to modify the style. When you select that option a dialog box will pop up with all of modification options you have available. You can change the font size and style, the paragraph formatting (if the style you are modifying can be applied to paragraphs), and even the name of the style.

You will also see a dropdown menu at the bottom of the sidebar that gives you options to see the available formatting and the formatting that is actually in use. This is a useful feature that will help you weed out styles that are not yet addressed.

Removing All Styles

One of the options in this Styles and Formatting sidebar is called "Clear Formatting." If your book was saved from PDF, InDesign, or Quark into Word you might want to remove all of the formatting and start with a clean slate. The easy way to do that is to select the text in the entire book (Ctrl + A) and click on "Clear Formatting" in the sidebar. The problem with this method is that you will not just lose your paragraph formatting; you will also lose any bold, italics, and underlines in the document.

If your book does not have a lot of that formatting or if you don't mind adding it back in manually, the Clear Formatting feature will certainly make the book easier to handle. However, I do not suggest using Clear Formatting on the whole book unless your book has way too many formatting issues to easily address.

Getting a Feel for the Book

You need to have a good feel for your book file before you get started. Take a quick look through the book and figure out the heading structure. Does your book only have chapter headings, or does it have subheadings, as well? If it has subheadings, how many levels does it have? It is a good idea to pull out a sheet of paper or open a new document and work out the structure of the book in an outline format. That will help you determine how and where to apply the heading styles.

Does your book have block indents? If so, are they formatted consistently with the same types of indentation or lack thereof? Are they italicized? Do they have footnotes or quotation references after them? Does your book have lists? Are they numbered or bulleted? What about tables and charts? How large are they? How are your images formatted? Are they floating to the right or left of paragraphs?

Initial Preparation

There are a couple of things you will want to do to get the book ready for further formatting and editing. First, decide whether you want to remove the "breadcrumb" header and footer content from the book. Since the Kindle does not have page numbers and the page headings are added automatically, the header and footer in your file are extraneous and can just add more styles to your list. The only caveat to this is that if your book has an index you will want to keep the page numbers. However, since the export to HTML ignores the header and footer content, you should move the page numbers into the main text at the appropriate spots and mark them somehow so that you can find them later. We will cover formatting indexes in more detail in Chapter 5.

Second, you should remove any images that are not needed in the final book, as well as any other content that is unnecessary. Doing this now can save you some time in the formatting stage.

Applying and Modifying Styles

There are two basic approaches to cleaning up your Word document and applying consistent styling. One approach is to go through the list of styles in the Styles and Formatting sidebar, modifying and merging them as necessary to whittle down the list. Another approach is to work your way through the book, applying new styles to each paragraph. I think a combination of these approaches is the best way to format a book in the shortest time possible.

So, since you know how the book is laid out and you are familiar with the formatting as it currently stands, you should make your way through the list of styles that are actually applied to the book and modify, remove, or merge them. When you click the arrow next to a style in the list and choose "Select all x instance(s)" you will then have the opportunity to change all of that formatting in one fell swoop. You can click on any other style in the list and the selected sections will be changed to follow that style, or you can click the down-arrow and modify the current style, give it a name, etc.

However, you should be careful because some of the styles in the list are applied to paragraphs and some are applied just to text within a paragraph. For example, if you have the program select all of the paragraphs with an "Arial 14 pt Black Centered Line spacing: single" style, then you click on the "Arial, 10pt" font style, all you will end up doing is creating an "Arial 10 pt Centered Line spacing: single" style. In other words, to overwrite one style with another you must overwrite paragraph styles with other paragraph styles, and font styles with other font styles.

The goal of this part of the process is to get your list of styles down to something manageable and also to ensure that each style is given a name. Both of these will make your HTML cleanup easier to manage. In all of this you should also remember that basic formatting is best. The Kindle has some built-in restrictions on formatting, so the less special formatting you add to your book the better it will turn out.

Since you have worked out the outline of your book, it should be easy to format the headings in a consistent way. It is best to name the heading styles as "Heading 1", "Heading 2," etc. They will come in very handy later if you make your Table of Contents in Word.

Choosing Your Next Step

Once you have cleaned up the formatting of your book and reduced the number of used styles down to a manageable size, you now have a decision to make: Are you going to convert the book into HTML and edit it some more, or are you going to continue working in the Word document. Some books, especially works of fiction, can usually be formatted just fine in Word. However, if your book has special formatting, lists, tables, images, an index, or even footnotes, you are going to be much better off formatting the book directly in HTML. This is especially true of books with images since the DTP will strip out the images when you upload.

If that is the case, you should skip to Chapter 3 and continue from there. Before you do, you will need to save your Word document as Filtered HTML. Just follow the instructions in Chapter 1, Word and RTF files on page 10.

Assuming you are moving forward with your formatting in Word, we are now going to discuss how to add some important features to your book.

Page Breaks in Word

Page breaks are very useful for breaking up the content in eBooks. They can be used to force chapters to begin on a new screen on the Kindle, to ensure that an image appears on a new screen, etc. To insert a page break using Word, just place your cursor in front of the paragraph you would like to force to the new page (such as a heading), hold down the Ctrl key on your keyboard, and press Enter. You can also go to the Insert menu, select "Break," ensure that "Page break" is selected, and click OK (Figure 2.7).

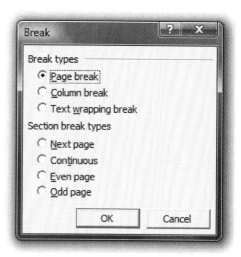

Figure 2.7

Table of Contents

Every eBook should have a Table of Contents (TOC), but unfortunately many authors and publishers don't include them. A TOC makes it easy for your readers to see where they are in the book and helps them navigate your content. Adding a TOC is easy to do in Word.

First, you'll need to make the TOC itself, a list at the front of your book to the major sections in the book text. The TOC should include all of the front matter (Preface, Introduction, etc.), the chapters, and any back matter (Epilogue, Appendix, Index, Footnotes, etc.). If your book is very long, the inclusion of a second level of headings can be useful for navigation; however, it is best to keep the TOC short and not include every level of subheadings that your book has. An index can be used to take the reader to more specific information.

After you have created the TOC list, it is time to link the items. Let's use the Preface as an example. Use your mouse or keyboard to select the word "Preface" in your TOC list. Go to the Insert menu and select Hyperlink (or press Ctrl + K). In the Hyperlink box (Figure 2.8), choose to add a link within the current file, and, if you marked up your book with heading styles as discussed above, you will be shown a tree structure of the headings in the book. Click on the Preface in that tree and click OK. The link to the Preface is now done.

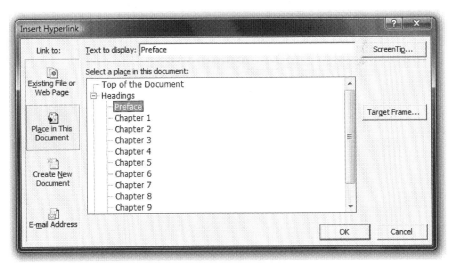

Figure 2.8

If you did not use heading styles you will need to add some bookmarks before you insert the hyperlinks. To insert bookmarks, scroll down to the place you want the link to go and place your cursor at the beginning of the paragraph. Go to the Insert menu and select Bookmark. In the Bookmark box, enter a name for your bookmark (for instance, "preface") and press OK. Now, when you add the hyperlink to the Preface, you will see "preface" in the tree list under bookmarks. This is the same process you should use to place anchors in the book for the page numbers and link the page numbers in the Index to the correct places.

Once your Table of Contents is complete, you also need to add a bookmark to the TOC heading itself. That will activate the link to the TOC in the Kindle book menu. Follow the instructions above and name the bookmark "TOC" in all-caps.

Moving Forward

If you want to work with the book in HTML and do further cleanup or formatting, save the Word document as Filtered HTML following the instructions in Chapter 1, Word and RTF files on page 10 and go on to Chapter 3. Otherwise, if you are ready to upload the book to the DTP, you can go to Chapter 8.

Chapter 3

Introduction to HTML

In my years as an eBook developer, I have met many authors without a technical bone in their body. I can see their eyes glazing over when I start using acronyms like HTML, XML, and CSS. While it may seem like these technologies are beyond your grasp, they really aren't. The average author may not want to learn the HTML language completely, but it is not too difficult to manage the process of editing your book in HTML using a few basic concepts.

Tools of the Trade

HTML editor

Before we get started with the HTML code, you will need to install a program that will assist you in your HTML editing process. There are quite a few programs available, including TextPad, Em Editor, UltraEdit, HTMLPad, Dreamweaver, and FrontPage. In addition, Windows comes with a built-in text editor called Notepad that can handle HTML editing in a pinch.

Despite the variety of for-sale options available, I am going to suggest that you download a free, Open Source HTML editor called Notepad++. Notepad++ can handle everything you will need to do to your files, while at the same time not getting in your way with extraneous features.

To download this program:

1. Go the Notepad++ website (http://notepad-plus.sourceforge.net).

2. Click on "Download" at the top of the page.

3. In the "Binary files" section at the top, select "Download Notepad++ executable files".

4. In the list you are given, choose the "npp.#.#.#.Installer.exe". The "#" represents the latest version number of the program, currently 5.1.4. If you see a later number available, choose it.

5. After the file has downloaded, install the program with the default options.

If you are working on a Macintosh, you can use Text Wrangler, or you can purchase a copy of TextMate if you are looking for more features. There are also other good Mac-compatible text/HTML editors available.

Regular Expressions

Throughout the rest of the book I will periodically offer suggestions for using Regular Expressions in your editing. Regular Expressions, often referred to as RegExes, are a find-and-replace "wildcard" language that makes editing HTML and other text-based languages much easier and faster. You can do the same tasks without RegExes, but it will usually take you much longer. I have included a list of common RegEx commands in Appendix B. It is also available in the Book Tools download on my website.

As a general introduction to RegExes, let's look at an example of how you might use them in your book editing. Let's say you want to add bookmarks to your chapter headings so that you can link your Table of Contents to the right places. In your HTML file the headings might look like this:

```
<h1>Chapter 1</h1>
<h1>Chapter 2</h1>
<h1>Chapter 3</h1>
```

To get the `<a name="chap#"/>` in front of each heading, you could just add it by hand; however, if your book has 40 chapters that would take a long time. Using the following RegEx in the find/replace box you can reduce that time considerably.

Find: (`<h1>Chapter `) (`[0-9]+`)

Replace: `<a name="chap\2"/>\1\2`

Notice that I am doing a search in the HTML for the heading tag, the word "Chapter" followed by a space, any number (`[0-9]`), and a plus sign, which means "one or more." I am grouping the results of the find statement into two parts using parentheses. That allows me to use the text found in those groups within my replace statement, referring to them as "\1" and "\2". When this RegEx is run on the entire book, it will replace all the current headings with this:

```
<a name="chap1"/><h1>Chapter 1</h1>
<a name="chap2"/><h1>Chapter 2</h1>
<a name="chap3"/><h1>Chapter 3</h1>
```

As you can see, Regular Expressions can be a powerful tool when you know how to use them. To learn more, you can look in the help files that come with your text editor or search for "Regular Expressions" online.

Perl

For the more technically-minded, the Perl programming language is also a powerful tool for formatting and preparing Kindle books. The details of how to use this programming language are outside the scope of this book, but Perl is a great language that was designed to manipulate text easily, and it allows you to use Regular Expressions in much more powerful ways than you can in any HTML editor.

Information on Perl programming is available in a wide range of books and online resources.

HTML Basics

HTML is a text-based language. This means that the foundation of the HTML file is the text itself. To show the structure of the document and give it formatting, you add markers (called "tags") to that foundational text. These tags are all written inside less-than (<) and greater-than (>) angle brackets, and the tag name itself tells the browser (or the Kindle) how to display the text.

All HTML tags should be opened and closed. An opening tag has the less-than angle bracket, the tag name, and the greater-than angle bracket—like this: <i>. The closing tag has the same parts, but has a forward slash before the tag name to indicate that it is being closed—like this: </i>. In some cases, the closing tag is merged with the opening tag, such as the break tag (<br/>) and the horizontal rule (<hr/>).

I have included a list of supported tags and styles in Appendix A, and there is a printable copy of the same information in the Book Tools download available on my website. Some examples·of common tags are:

<h1>, <h2>, ... <h6> — Heading tags, used to format chapter headings and subheadings.

<p> — Paragraph tag, used to format regular paragraphs

<i> — Italics

<b> — Bold

You can extend the functionality and formatting abilities of these tags by adding attributes with values to them. For instance, let's say you wanted to add a margin above your <h1> tag. To do that in a way that the Kindle understands, you will add a height attribute with a value of 30 pixels, like this: <h1 height="30">. Or, if you wanted to make your paragraph not have a first-line indent you would use this attribute/value: <p width="0">.

I highly suggest that you look over the list of tags that are supported in the Kindle and become familiar with what they can do. We will discuss them in depth in Chapter 5.

CSS

Cascading Style Sheets (CSS) work much in the same way as the Styles function in Word. They allow you to make sweeping style changes across the HTML file, applying styles to all of your paragraphs, headings, or other elements in one place. That makes your entire formatting process easier and quicker.

A CSS style consists of the name of the HTML tag that the styles should be applied to followed by the list of styles inserted between curly brackets and separated by semicolons, like this:

```
blockquote {
     font-weight: bold;
     font-size: small;
}
p.center {
     text-align: center;
}
```

A formula for CSS would look like this:

```
HTMLtagName.ClassName {
     StyleName1: Value;
     StyleName2: Value;
     StyleName3: Value;
}
```

A "class name" is a way to apply the same style to a large number of HTML tags at once. For instance, if you wanted to make a centered paragraph using the style above, you could code the HTML like this:

```
<p class="center">This is centered
text.</p>
```

You could then re-use the `class="center"` style throughout the book on any paragraph you want to center. You could also remove the HTML tag name from the front of the CSS reference, starting it with the period, and making the style available for use on other HTML tags besides `<p>` tags.

We will cover CSS in more detail in Chapters 5 and 6. The HTML reference in Appendix A gives a list of CSS elements that are supported in the Kindle (see page 143).

I suggest that you place all your CSS in

```
<style type="text/css">
    /* styles go here */
</style>
```

tags at the top of your HTML document, not in a separate style sheet file or inline within your book. That will allow you to easily edit the styles as you work and will mitigate any issues the DTP has with multiple files.

Chapter 4

HTML Cleanup

In this chapter we will talk about cleaning up your HTML code and making it easier for the DTP to use. If you formatted your book in Microsoft Word as I described in Chapter 2, this step in the process will be much less work than if you are attempting to clean up HTML generated by PDF or from an un-edited Word document.

Messy HTML

What do I mean by "messy HTML"? Well, most books that are converted into HTML from Word or PDF have much more formatting included in them than they actually require. This extraneous formatting will cause all sorts of formatting issues in the Kindle and can make the clean-up job extremely difficult. Let's take a look at a few examples of messy code that you might see.

Word HTML

While Microsoft Word can (as described in Chapter 2) be forced to make some decent HTML by using the Styles function, most Word documents are not formatted with Styles. The end result of regular Word markup converted into HTML is a lot of extraneous `<span>` tags and specific formatting that has no equivalent in the Kindle. Here is an example of that formatting:

```
<h1 align=center style='margin-
top:.25in;margin-right:0in;margin-
bottom:0in;
```

```
margin-left:0in;margin-
bottom:.0001pt;text-align:center'><span
style='font-size:20.0pt;color:black'>PART
ONE </span></h1>
<h3 align=center style='margin-
top:6.0pt;margin-right:0in;margin-
bottom:6.0pt;
margin-left:0in;text-align:center'><span
style='color:black'>CHAPTER I </span></h3>
<h3 align=center style='margin-
top:6.0pt;margin-right:0in;margin-
bottom:12.0pt;
margin-left:0in;text-
align:center'><i><span
style='color:black'>A SHIFTING REEF
</span></i></h3>
<p style='margin:0in;margin-
bottom:.0001pt;text-align:justify'><span
style='font-size:13.5pt;color:black'>The
year 1866 was signalised by a
remarkable incident, a mysterious and
puzzling phenomenon, which doubtless no
one has yet forgotten. Not to mention
rumours which agitated the maritime
population and excited the public mind,
even in the interior of continents,
seafaring men were particularly excited.
Merchants, common sailors, captains of
vessels, skippers, both of Europe and
America, naval officers of all countries,
and the Governments of several States on
the two continents, were deeply
interested in the matter. </span></p>
<p style='margin:0in;margin-
bottom:.0001pt;text-align:justify'><span
style='font-size:13.5pt;color:black'>For
some time past vessels had been met by
"an enormous thing," a long object,
spindle-shaped, occasionally
phosphorescent, and infinitely larger and
more rapid in its movements than a
whale. </span></p>
```

Notice that the Headings and paragraphs all have margins and other styles in the `style` attribute, and that there are other styles like font size and color added to the span tags. Here is what that same text would look like when it is cleaned up:

```
<h1>PART ONE</h1>
<h3>CHAPTER I</h3>
<h3><i>A SHIFTING REEF</i></h3>
<p>The year 1866 was signalised by a
remarkable incident, a mysterious and
puzzling phenomenon, which doubtless no
one has yet forgotten. Not to mention
rumours which agitated the maritime
population and excited the public mind,
even in the interior of continents,
seafaring men were particularly excited.
Merchants, common sailors, captains of
vessels, skippers, both of Europe and
America, naval officers of all countries,
and the Governments of several States on
the two continents, were deeply interested
in the matter.</p>
<p>For some time past vessels had been met
by &ldquo;an enormous thing,&rdquo; a long
object, spindle-shaped, occasionally
phosphorescent, and infinitely larger and
more rapid in its movements than a
whale.</p>
```

As you can tell, this code is much cleaner and easier to understand. The formatting has been trimmed down, and all the extraneous styles and tags have been removed.

PDF HTML

Adobe PDF files create HTML that is even more bloated and messy than Word. I took the same Word document we used above, created a PDF from it using Adobe Acrobat, and exported it as HTML from Acrobat. Here is what it gave me:

```
<H1 ID="LinkTarget_21">
<SPAN style="color:#000000"
```

```
>PART ONE </SPAN
><SPAN style="font-size:24pt;
color:#000000"
> </SPAN
></H1>
<H3 ID="LinkTarget_22">
<SPAN style="font-size:13.5pt;
color:#000000"
>CHAPTER I  </SPAN
></H3>
<H3 ID="LinkTarget_23" style="margin-
bottom:16px">
<SPAN style="font-size:13.5pt; font-
style:italic; color:#000000"
>A SHIFTING REEF </SPAN
><SPAN style="font-size:13.5pt;
color:#000000"
> </SPAN
></H3>
<P>
<SPAN style="font-size:13.5pt; font-
weight:normal; color:#000000"
>The year 1866 wa</SPAN
><SPAN style="font-size:13.5pt; font-
weight:normal; color:#000000"
>s signalised by a remarkable incident, a
mysterious and puzzling phenomenon, which
doubtless no one has yet forgotten. Not to
mention rumours which agitated the
maritime population and excited the public
mind, even in the interior of continents,
seafaring men were particularly excited.
Merchants, common sailors, captains of
vessels, skippers, both of Europe and
America, naval officers of all countries,
and the Governments of several States on
the two continents, were deeply interested
in the matter. </SPAN
><SPAN style="font-size:12pt; font-
weight:normal; color:#000000"
> </SPAN
></P>
```

```
<P>
<SPAN style="font-size:13.5pt; font-
weight:normal; color:#000000"
>For some time past vessels had been met
by â€œan enormous thing,â€  a long object,
spindle-shaped, occasionally
phosphorescent, and infinitely larger and
more rapid in its movements than a whale.
</SPAN
><SPAN style="font-size:12pt; font-
weight:normal; color:#000000"
> </SPAN
></P>
```

There are a lot of differences between this output and the Word output above. First, there is a lot more code added to the file. There are more <span> tags, more attributes, and even some added ids. Second, the line breaks are added inside the tags themselves and at odd places. Third, the curly quotes (" and "), which were fine in the Word document, came over as garbled text from the PDF (â€œ and â€).

These differences can cause many problems as you try to clean up the code and make it more useable. This is why I suggest that you convert the PDF to Word before converting to HTML. When you go that route, the code may look something like this:

```
<h1 align=center style='margin-
top:.25in;text-align:center'> <b><span
style='font-size:20.0pt;color:black'>PART
ONE </span></b><b><span
style='font-
size:24.0pt;color:black'> </span></b></h1>
<h3 align=center style='margin-
top:6.0pt;margin-right:0in;margin-
bottom:6.0pt;
margin-left:0in;text-
align:center'><b><span style='font-
size:13.5pt;color:black'>CHAPTER
I </span></b></h3>
```

```
<h3 align=center style='margin-
top:6.0pt;margin-right:0in;margin-
bottom:9.65pt;
margin-left:0in;text-
align:center'><b><i><span style='font-
size:13.5pt;
color:black'>A SHIFTING REEF
</span></i></b><b><span style='font-
size:13.5pt;
color:black'> </span></b></h3>
<p style='text-align:justify;text-
indent:24.0pt'><span style='font-
size:13.5pt;
color:black'>The year 1866 was signalised
by a remarkable incident, a
mysterious and puzzling phenomenon, which
doubtless no one has yet forgotten.
Not to mention rumours which agitated the
maritime population and excited the
public mind, even in the interior of
continents, seafaring men were
particularly excited. Merchants, common
sailors, captains of vessels, skippers,
both of Europe and America, naval officers
of all countries, and the
Governments of several States on the two
continents, were deeply interested in
the matter. </span><span style='font-
size:11.5pt;color:black'> </span></p>
<p class=Default style='text-
align:justify;text-indent:24.0pt'><span
style='font-size:13.5pt'>For some time
past vessels had been met by "an
enormous thing," a long object, spindle-
shaped, occasionally phosphorescent,
and infinitely larger and more rapid in
its movements than a whale. </span><span
style='font-size:11.5pt'> </span></p>
```

This HTML is not exactly like the code we got from Word directly, but it is certainly cleaner than the HTML we got from the PDF.

Mobipocket HTML

Mobipocket Creator does a better job of creating clean HTML, but it also has some issues of which you should be aware.

```
<b><font size="+3">PART ONE</font><br/>
CHAPTER I   <br/>
<i>A SHIFTING REEF </i></b>
<p>The year 1866 was signalised by a
remarkable incident, a mysterious and
puzzling phenomenon, which doubtless no
one has yet forgotten. Not to mention
rumours which agitated the maritime
population and excited the public mind,
even in
the interior of continents, seafaring men
were particularly excited. Merchants,
common sailors, captains of vessels,
skippers, both of Europe and America,
naval
officers of all countries, and the
Governments of several States on the two
continents,
were deeply interested in the matter. </p>
<p>For some time past vessels had been met
by &ldquo;an enormous thing,&rdquo; a long
object,
spindle-shaped, occasionally
phosphorescent, and infinitely larger and
more rapid in
its movements than a whale. </p>
```

Notice that the bloat is all gone, but the heading is not in a heading tag and there are some other issues that will make formatting a bit harder to do. Overall, though, the code could be much easier to work with.

Joining Paragraph Lines

One thing you may have noticed in the above examples, and which you will see in your own file after you convert it into HTML, is that there are line breaks added throughout the file. These line breaks are not a problem for HTML since it will only start a new paragraph when you have a `<p>` tag; however, they do make editing the file more difficult, especially if you are using regular expressions and making a lot of changes to your file.

The easiest way to remove these line breaks is to create a Perl script that will do the work for you, and run it on your file. Here is a simple script that will work well for that purpose:

```perl
#!/usr/bin/perl
my $book;
my $in = "MyBook.html";
my $out = "MyBook.linebreaksremoved.html";
{
    open IN, $in;
    local $/;
    $book = <IN>;
}
$book =~ s{(<body.*</body>)}{
    my $body=$1;
    $body =~ s{<(p|h[1-
6]|td|li|dt|dd).*?</\1>}{
      $all = $&;
      $all =~ s/\n/ /g;
      $all =~ s/\s\s+/ /g;
      $all;
    }gesi;
    while ($body =~ s{\n\n}{\n}g) {}
    "$body";
}esi;
open OUT, ">$out";
print OUT $book;
```

This script is also available in the Book Tools section on my website.

Removing Extraneous Styles and Tags

The next step in cleaning up your document is to remove the unneeded styles and tags that were inserted by Word or Acrobat. Which styles and tags you remove will be completely up to you, but I highly suggest that you strip the

HTML down to its most basic tags. Doing so will remedy most display problems and make the book consistent throughout.

As you are stripping out extra tags and styles, you will want to replace them with tags and formatting that work well in the Kindle. For instance, if all of your chapter headings look like this:

```
<p align=center style='margin-
top:.25in;text-align:center'><b><span
style='font-
size:20.0pt;color:black'>Chapter 1
</span></b><b><span style='font-
size:24.0pt;color:black'> </span></b></p>
```

you will want to turn them into actual heading tags in the HTML file, like this:

```
<h1>Chapter 1</h1>
```

If you only turn that into a regular paragraph (`<p>Chapter 1</p>`) you will have to go back later and change it into a heading during the formatting stage. In other words, you need to think out your book layout a little bit before starting your cleanup, and you need to know what you want to do with the elements of your book before you completely remove a style. To that end, I highly suggest that you read Chapter 5 before starting on your cleanup so you will know what tags and styles will work.

The majority of tags and styles present in your file will actually be helpful in your efforts to convert the file to clean, Kindle-ready HTML. You can use unneeded styles like margins to help you give headings the right spacing, or to find places where your file has a blank line between paragraphs to show a scene change. The difficulty is that there are most likely also margins in your file that are really not needed. Discerning what to use and what to remove will require some investigation.

When I am cleaning up a file I usually start with the easy pickings, like the regular paragraphs. In most books the paragraphs just need to be formatted as a `<p>` tag, but you will probably see something more like one of these examples in your HTML:

```
<p class=MsoNormal style='line-
height:24.0pt;text-autospace:none'><span
style='font-size:14.0pt'>
```

```
<p class=MsoNormal style='margin-
left:40.3pt;text-align:justify;line-
height:150%;text-autospace:none'><span
style='line-height:150%;font-family:Times-
Roman'>
```

```
<p class=MsoNormalCxSpMiddle style='text-
indent:.5in;line-height:normal'><span
lang=EN-CA style='font-size:10.0pt;font-
family:Arial;color:black'>
```

```
<p class=MsoNormal><span style='font-
size:12.0pt'>
```

Notice the variety in formatting. All of that is due to the settings used by the authors when they were formatting their books in Word. In most books, changing these to `<p>` tags will make the book code much more manageable. Be careful to ensure that the tags you replace are actually the regular paragraphs, not a specially styled paragraph, a poem, or something else. You will want to handle those individually.

Next, it is usually best to attack the chapter headings, and any subheadings your book may have. Just as with paragraphs, you may find a variety of styles applied to headings. The main difference is that they will probably not be as consistent as the paragraphs to replace. You may find that searching in the HTML file for "Chapter" is the easiest way to find them all. You may also notice a pattern in the font size formatting for the various headings, such as all top-level (chapter) headings being formatted in "`font-size:20.0pt;`" and all the second-level subheadings being formatted in "`font-size:16.0pt;`". The key, as in all of the cleanup process, is to look for patterns and put them to good use.

In that vein, let's work out a RegEx that might come in handy with your headings. Say you have a chapter heading like this one:

```
<p align=center style='margin-
top:.25in;text-align:center'><b><span
style='font-
size:20.0pt;color:black'>Chapter 1
</span></b></p>
```

but when you look at Chapter 2 you see that it is slightly different, with a top margin of .50in. To catch both of these in one fell swoop, you will want to create a RegEx that ignores the top margin and bases its search on something else that you know is standardized, like the font-size. Here is an example of what that could look like:

Find: `<p[^>]*><b><span[^>]+font-size:20.0pt[^>]*>(Chapter [^<]+)</span></b></p>`

Replace: `<h1>\1</h2>`

Of course, there are other RegExes you can use in a situation like this, but that should give you the general idea.

The next step I usually take is to get rid of all the span tags, since they are the worst bloat-creators in program-generated HTML. You will want to search for "<span" in your book, and deal with each type of span tag individually. When you notice a pattern, use a RegEx to convert the span tag into something usable.

When you have finished those three pieces of your process, you have probably handled the majority of the basic cleanup your file needs. Now it is time to learn about the formatting that the Kindle supports and how to make your book look great on the device.

Chapter 5

Formatting Your Book

While the Kindle format is essentially HTML, the device only supports a small portion of the tags and styles that are supported in most Web browsers and other HTML viewers. That actually works out well for you as an author or publisher, since it removes some complexity from the formatting process.

In this chapter I will cover the HTML tags and styles that work in the Kindle. I have also included a list of supported tags and styles in Appendix A, and there is a printable copy of the same information in the Book Tools section of my website.

Font Formatting

To start out, let's take a look at some of the basic text formatting tools you have at your disposal.

Bold and Italics

To make text bold in your book, you will need to apply the <b> tag, and to italicize text in your book, you will need to apply the <i> tag. For example:

```
I entered, and found <b>Captain Nemo</b>
deep in algebraical calculations of
<i>x</i> and <i>other</i> quantities.
```

> I entered, and found Captain Nemo deep in algebraical calculations of *x* and *other* quantities.

You can also apply bold to any tag in your style sheet using the `font-weight: bold;` property, and italics using the `text-style: italic;` property.

The `<em>` tag and `<strong>` tag are often thought of as replacements for the `<b>` and `<i>` tags. These tags are intended for use in specific situations when the text being marked up requires *emphasis* or **strong emphasis**. Like most browsers, the Kindle will format `<em>` as italics and `<strong>` as bold.

Underline

To underline text in the Kindle, use the `<u>` tag.

```
Henry, O. <u>The Four Million</u>. New
York: McClure, Phillips &amp; Co., 1906.
```

> Henry, O. <u>The Four Million</u>. New York: McClure, Phillips & Co., 1906.

You can also apply an underline style to any tag in your style sheet using the `text-decoration: underline;` property.

Big and Small

There are times when making some text bigger or smaller than the default size is necessary. While the Kindle does allow a small amount of tweaking with the CSS `font-size` property, the easiest and most consistent way to adjust font sizes in your text is by using the `<big>` and `<small>` tags. These tags can also be nested to enhance the effect.

Three examples of the use of `<big>` and `<small>` come to mind. The first using the `<big>` tag to create a drop cap of sorts. Since the Kindle does not allow floating elements, the large letter will not actually "drop," but the overall effect is similar. For example:

```
<p><big><big><big>T</big></big></big>here
were two or three things...</p>
```

There were two or three things...

The second example is using the `<small>` tag on a copyright page. I do this by default in most of my books because it more closely matches most hardcopies.

```
<p><small><i>The Four Million</i>,
copyright &copy; 1906 by O.
Henry.</small></p>
```

The third example is using the `<small>` tag to create the impression of small caps. The default font of the Kindle does not, unfortunately, allow the use of small caps, but to give the same effect just put `<small>` tags around the small caps text, like this:

```
W<small>ILLIAM</small>
S<small>YDNEY</small>
P<small>ORTER</small>
```

WILLIAM SYDNEY PORTER

Superscript and Subscript

The Kindle displays superscripted and subscripted text using the `<sup>` and `<sub>` tags. The text inside those tags is not only shifted up or down on the line, it is also reduced in size. The `<sup>` tag is most commonly used to format footnote numbers, like this:

```
Jules Verne makes his story more
believable by setting the events in his
own time.<a href="#note1"><sup>1</sup></a>
```

Jules Verne makes his story more believable by setting the events in his own time.[1]

The `<a>` tag around this footnote will be explained on page 113.

The `<sup>` and `<sub>` tags can both be used to create consistently-styled fractions. The line height of the line with the fraction on it will be expanded a bit, but the overall effect looks pretty good despite that.

```
The story was <sup>1</sup>/<sub>2</sub> as
long as the author intended.
```

> The story was $^1/_2$ as long as the author intended.

Note that the Kindle does not allow tweaking of the `line-height` CSS property or the `vertical-align` property, so there is no way to adjust the placement of the superscripted or subscripted text. It also does not allow you to change the size of the characters in the `<sup>` or `<sub>` tags.

Strikethrough

There are two HTML tags that allow you to strike out some text (place a line through it): the `<s>` and `<strike>` tags. These both look exactly the same on the Kindle.

```
<p><s>strikethrough text</s></p>
<p>this is <s>strikethrough text</s></p>
```

> ~~strikethrough text~~
>
> this is ~~strikethrough text~~

This image also shows a small bug in the implementation of the formatting on the Kindle screen. In the first example, because the text of the entire paragraph is formatted in a strikethrough tag *and* because that text is the first text on the page, the first word is not given the strikethrough style. If there were a single character before the `<s>` tag the bug would not be present.

On the Kindle 2 the placement of the strikethrough line has changed. It now shows up closer to the middle of the word than it does on the Kindle 1. Notice that the same formatting bug is present in the Kindle 2.

> ~~strikethrough text~~
> this is ~~strikethrough text~~

You can also apply a strikethrough style to any tag in your style sheet using the `text-decoration: line-through;` property.

Span Tags

The `<span>` tag is a multi-purpose tag that does not apply any style of its own to the text. Instead, it is used to apply styles from a style sheet or inline styles to the text it surrounds. As we discussed at the beginning of Chapter 4, `<span>` tags are over-used by programs like Word and Acrobat, being strewn throughout a file to assign styles that would be better applied elsewhere.

There are not many cases where a `<span>` tag will become necessary in your book. Most of the styles you will be applying have tags of their own. However, it is available if you find the need to use it.

Code and Other Mono-spaced Text

Coinciding with the release of the Kindle 2, the Kindle 1 firmware was updated to support the use of a mono-spaced font. This is very useful for inserting computer code into a book, just like I do throughout this one. To apply this style, you will need to wrap the text in one of the following tags: `<code>`, `<kbd>`, `<samp>`, or `<tt>`.

```
This is CODE text
This is KBD text
This is SAMP text
This is TT text
```

The Kindle **does not** support the use of the CSS style `font-family: monospace;` for applying a mono-spaced font. That means all of your mono-spaced text must be in one of the above tags.

Also, the `<pre>` tag does not work on the Kindle.

Paragraphs

The Kindle supports six main types of paragraph formatting:

- **Normal:** The Kindle applies a standardized first-line indent and full justification to every paragraph.
- **No-indent:** This will override the first-line indent and make that line flush left.
- **Left-aligned:** This will override the default full justification and make the right edge of the paragraphs jagged.
- **Right-aligned:** Text will be aligned on the right of the screen and the left edge will be jagged.
- **Centered:** Text will be centered on the screen.
- **Hanging:** You can use hanging indents to make poetry, bibliographies, and even lists.

Let's discuss these formatting options in detail.

Default Paragraph Formatting

When you place a `<p>` tag in your HTML file the Kindle will apply some default formatting to it. This was most likely done in an effort to make every book seem more consistent on the screen, but it has led to some consternation among those of us who format Kindle books because it means you have to override the formatting explicitly in your file if you don't want it to be applied. Thankfully, the ability to override some of the default formatting does exist.

The default formatting that is applied to regular paragraphs is a consistent line height, a first-line indent that stays at 0.25 inches (about 0.6 cm) regardless of the font size chosen by the user, and justified paragraph formatting (which means that the text is aligned both on the left and right of the screen). Of those three styles, the line height is the only one that cannot be overridden in the code (though, on the Kindle 2, users have the ability to specify the line height they want using the Alt + Number shortcuts). We will discuss the other two styles in the sections to follow.

You can apply a larger first-line indent to your paragraphs if you think that the 0.25 inch indent is not enough. To do that, use the `width` attribute in your paragraph tag like this:

```
<p width="75">There were two or three
things that I wanted to know. I do not
care about a mystery....</p>
```

The value in the `width` attribute can be in:

pixels (`width="40"`),
points (`width="40pt"`),
percent (`width="10%"`),
or *em*-units (`width="2em"`).

A Note about Measurements

The Kindle accepts four common measurements in its `width` and `height` attributes and in certain CSS attributes. These four measurements are pixels, points, percent, and *em*-units. The pixel and point measurements are treated exactly the same on the screen, so I usually just use the pixels. When you use pixels in the `width` and `height` attributes, you should not include "px" or "pixels" in the value — just give it a number with no units (e.g., `width="30"`).

Percent will apply a percentage of the screen measurement to the attribute. I have seen this unit of measurement be a little bit unpredictable, so it might be best to leave it alone.

Em-units are generally defined as the full height of the font being used. In web browsers an *em* is a variable unit that expands and contracts with the font size, but on the Kindle the *em* has a static size. The real problem, however, is that the measurement is different on the Kindle 1 and the Kindle 2. On the Kindle 1, an *em* is 1/4 of an inch, while on Kindle 2 it is 1/8 of an inch.

As you see on the next page, this difference in size can make a big difference in the formatting. Figure 5.1 shows how the Kindle 1 displays *em*s and Figure 5.2 shows how Kindle 2 does.

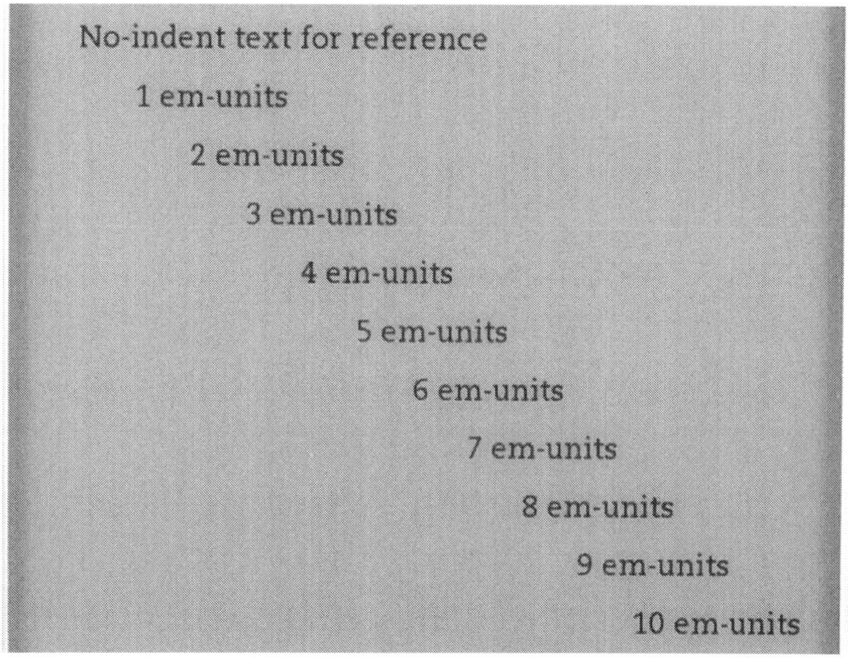

No-indent text for reference

1 em-units

2 em-units

3 em-units

4 em-units

5 em-units

6 em-units

7 em-units

8 em-units

9 em-units

10 em-units

Figure 5.1

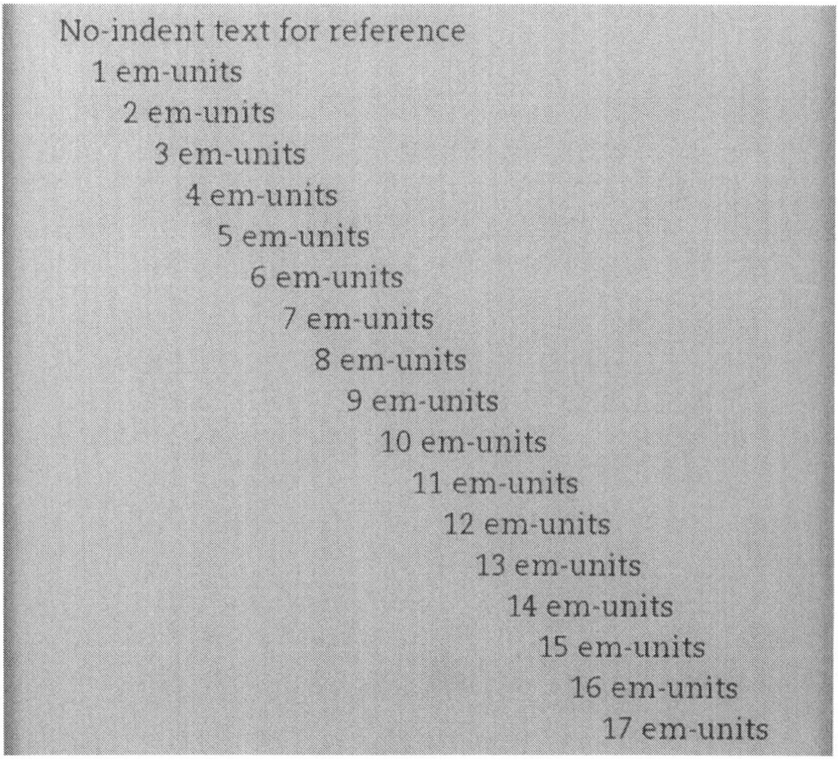

No-indent text for reference

1 em-units

2 em-units

3 em-units

4 em-units

5 em-units

6 em-units

7 em-units

8 em-units

9 em-units

10 em-units

11 em-units

12 em-units

13 em-units

14 em-units

15 em-units

16 em-units

17 em-units

Figure 5.2

Pixels are a stable measurement on both devices, so I suggest you stick with them unless or until Amazon fixes these differences.

No-indent Paragraphs

To override the default first-line indent applied by the Kindle, you can choose to use a CSS rule or an in-line `width` command. I suggest using the CSS rule since it is easier to adjust later if the need arises. Let's say you want to apply a no-indent rule to every paragraph that follows a heading. You can assign a class name to the paragraphs you want to change and give that class the "`text-indent:0;`" style in the `<style>` tag at the top of the book. For instance:

```
<style type="text/css">
p.noind {
   text-indent: 0;
}
</style>
. . . . . . . . . .
<h1>Man About Town</h1>
<p class="noind">There were two or three
things that I wanted to know....</p>
```

If you wanted to make that change to the HTML file easily, you could use a regular expression like this one:

Find: `</h1>\n<p>`

Replace: `</h1>\n<p class="noind">`

To apply the no-indent style to one paragraph without using CSS, assign the paragraph a `width="0"` attribute like this:

```
<p width="0">There were two or three
things that I wanted to know....</p>
```

Notice how the difference in *em*-units display affects the book indentation in these photos of the Kindle 1 (left) and Kindle 2 (right). You can also easily see the difference in default line heights.

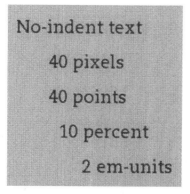

What if you wanted to apply the no-indent style to all of the paragraphs in your book? You could do it by taking out the class name from the style example given above, like this:

```
<style type="text/css">
p {
  text-indent: 0;
}
</style>
```

However, that may have unintended consequences on your book layout. You could also assign the `<p class="noind">` class to all the regular `<p>` tags in your book. That would be a little bit more targeted. If you do assign the no-indent rule across the book, you should take a look at the section on margins on page 68 to learn how to give your paragraphs a top margin so that the text does not run together too much.

Left-Aligned Paragraphs

The Kindle assigns a default full justification to all of the paragraphs in the book. This means that text will be aligned flush with both the right and left margins of the screen. Sometimes this formatting makes the text on a line spread out with lots of space between words, especially when a long word or a hyperlink is forced to wrap to the next line. Of course, this effect will vary depending on what font size the user is reading the book in. On the Kindle 1 this justification can also be turned off by the user for all books in a special, hidden command (Alt + J in the Font Size menu). This feature is not available on the Kindle 2.

If you want to override this formatting in your book, you can assign the "text-align: left;" style as desired. For example:

```
<style type="text/css">
p.left {
   text-align: left;
}
</style>
. . . . . . . . . .
<h1>Chapter 1</h1>
<p class="left">There were two or three
things that I wanted to know. I do not
care about a mystery. So I began to
inquire.</p>
```

Of course, you could also combine that with the no-indent style discussed above to remove the default first-line indent.

To assign the left-align style to an individual paragraph you can add the following attribute to the paragraph tag: `<p align="left">`.

Example of left-aligned text.

of knowledge was enlightenment concerning the character known as A Man About Town. He was more vague in my mind than a type should be. We must have a concrete idea of anything, even if it be an imaginary idea, before we can comprehend it. Now, I have a mental picture of John Doe that is as clear as a steel engraving. His eyes are weak blue; he wears a brown vest and a shiny black serge coat. He stands always in the sunshine chewing something; and he keeps half-shutting his pocket knife and opening it again with his thumb. And, if the Man Higher Up is ever found, take my assurance for it, he will be a large, pale man with blue wristlets showing under his cuffs, and he will be sitting to have his shoes polished within sound of a bowling alley, and there will be

Locations 14-19  OFF   Menu ▶

Right-Aligned Paragraphs

Sometimes you will want a paragraph to be aligned on the right side of the screen. I have found that this works well for signature lines at the end of a Foreword or Preface. To do this, you will assign the "text-align: right;" rule to the paragraphs. For example:

```
<style type="text/css">
p.right {
  text-align: right;
}
</style>
. . . . . . . . . .
<p class="right">Very Sincerely Yours,</p>
<p class="right">O. Henry</p>
<p class="right">New York, 1906</p>
```

Very Sincerely Yours,

O. Henry

New York, 1906

It is important to remember that the first-line indent style will still be applied to these paragraphs. That extra quarter of an inch can make a big difference in longer paragraphs, so you might want to apply the no-indent style explained above to remove the first-line indent.

To assign the right-align style to an individual paragraph you can add the following attribute to the paragraph tag: <p align="right">.

Centered Paragraphs

To center a paragraph on the screen, use the "text-align: center;" CSS rule. For example:

```
<style type="text/css">
.center {
  text-align: center;
}
</style>
```

```
. . . . . . . . . .
<h1 class="center">Man About Town</p>
<p class="center">by</p>
<p class="center"><b>O. Henry</b></p>
```

Man About Town

by

O. Henry

You can also assign the center-align style to an individual paragraph by adding the following attribute to the paragraph tag: `<p align="center">`.

One more way to center content is to use the `<center>` tag. This tag can be placed outside of `<h1>` and `<p>` tags like this:

```
<center>
<h1>Man About Town</p>
<p class="noind">by</p>
<p class="noind"><b>O. Henry</b></p>
</center>
```

Notice that the paragraphs in this example should still have the first-line indent removed (in this case, with the "noind" class we discussed above). Overall, I find the `<center>` tag to be much less powerful than using basic CSS to achieve the same effect.

Hanging Paragraphs

Hanging indents are very useful in the Kindle. Not only can they be used to format poetry and bibliographies, they can also be used to create pseudo-lists that are not indented as far as regular lists are on the Kindle (more on that later). A basic hanging indent utilizes the `width` attribute, the same attribute you can use to format the first-line indent on a paragraph. The only difference is that hanging indents use a negative value. For instance:

```
<p width="-30">Henry, O. <i>The Four
Million</i>. New York: McClure, Phillips
&amp; Co., 1906.</p>
```

Henry, O. *The Four Million*. New York: McClure,

Phillips & Co., 1906.

The value in the width attribute can be in:

pixels (width="-30"),
points (width="-10pt"),
percent (width="-10%"),
or *em*-units (width="-3em").

Note that the text-indent CSS property will not accept a negative number, so you cannot create a CSS style that applies these hanging indents. You must use the width attribute.

Poetry

The width attribute is actually a relatively unknown option in Kindle formatting. Some authors have instead tried to use <blockquote> tags to format poetry, but that only makes the poetry indent too far and become hard to read. Using the width attribute and some non-breaking spaces, I have worked out a great system for displaying up to six indentation levels of poetry, all with hanging indents, and all with nice formatting at any font size.

Here is an example of the formatting applied to the first stanza of "She Walks in Beauty" by Lord Byron:

```
<p width="-30">She walks in beauty, like
the night</p>
<p width="-
60">     Of
cloudless climes and starry skies;</p>
<p width="-30">And all that's best of dark
and bright</p>
<p width="-
60">     Meet in
her aspect and her eyes:</p>
```

```
<p width="-30">Thus mellowed to that
tender light</p>
<p width="-
60">     Which
heaven to gaudy day denies.</p>
```

> She walks in beauty, like the night
>
> Of cloudless climes and starry skies;
>
> And all that's best of dark and bright
>
> Meet in her aspect and her eyes:
>
> Thus mellowed to that tender light
>
> Which heaven to gaudy day denies.

Notice that the second level of indentation uses 5 non-breaking spaces to force the first line over. Those non-breaking spaces are used in all of the other levels to get the indentation correctly formatted.

The six levels are:

```
<p width="-30">
<p width="-60">[with 5  ]
<p width="-90">[with 10  ]
<p width="-120">[with 15  ]
<p width="-150">[with 20  ]
<p width="-180">[with 25  ]
```

The greatest feature of this special formatting is that when the lines wrap, they are indented to the middle distance between the current paragraph indentation and the next level of indentation. This makes poetry much easier to read, and can be useful in other situations, as you will see later.

Break Tags

In addition to regular paragraph tags, the Kindle allows the use of <br/> tags. These tags will break the text in a paragraph and force the content following it to a new line. Since a new paragraph is not being created, the same paragraph formatting applied to the parent paragraph, such as center- or right-alignment, will still be applied after the `<br/>`. However, since the new line is not the first line of the paragraph, any width or no-indent style will not be applied, and the text will act as if it just wrapped to the next line.

Unlike in regular HTML, there is no difference in the line height or margins applied to a paragraph with `<br/>` tags.

Some designers use `<br/>` tags to create margins around paragraphs or headings. While doing so will get the job done, I do suggest that you use the margin formatting described on page 68 instead.

Notice that the `<br/>` tag has the closing slash we talked about on page 28. While it is not required, it is the preferred practice in XHTML.

Division Tags

`<div>` tags are normally used in HTML to divide the contents of the document into sections. These tags are very useful for doing page layout on websites, but on the Kindle they effectively become just another form of `<p>` tag. You can apply the same styles and formatting described above to the `<div>` tag.

Block Quotes

One commonly used text format is the block quote. Offical writing style guides (Turabian, MLA, APA, Chicago, etc.) differ slightly on when block quotes should be used, but the general rule is that they should be used whenever the text being quoted is longer than just a snippet quoted in a sentence.

In regular HTML, multiple paragraphs can be included in the same `<blockquote>` tag. On the Kindle, however, if you have `<p>` tags inside a `<blockquote>` the `<blockquote>` will be completely ignored and the regular paragraph style will be applied. To make block quotes on the Kindle, then, you must remove the paragraph tags and use `<blockquote>` tags in their place. For example:

```
<p>The man from the West unfolded the
little piece of paper handed him. His hand
was steady when he began to read, but it
trembled a little by the time he had
finished. The note was rather short.</p>
   <blockquote>Bob: I was at the appointed
   place on time. When you struck the match
   to light your cigar I saw it was the
   face of the man wanted in Chicago.
   Somehow I couldn't do it myself, so I
   went around and got a plain clothes man
   to do the job.</blockquote>
   <p class="right">JIMMY</p>
```

> The man from the West unfolded the little piece of paper handed him. His hand was steady when he began to read, but it trembled a little by the time he had finished. The note was rather short.
>
> > Bob: I was at the appointed place on time. When you struck the match to light your cigar I saw it was the face of the man wanted in Chicago. Somehow I couldn't do it myself, so I went around and got a plain clothes man to do the job.
> >
> > JIMMY

On the Kindle 1, the `<blockquote>` tag gives the entire block of text a 0.5 inch left margin, but no right margin. On the Kindle 2 it gives the text a 0.25 inch left margin. The `<blockquote>` tag does not assign a first-line indent, but you can give it one by using the `width` property as described on page 51. You can also make the text left-aligned, right-aligned, and centered, and the text will still keep its left margin. However, it is not possible to assign a hanging indent to a <blockquote>; it will just be treated like a paragraph.

Block quotes can be used to create progressive indentation by nesting the block quote tags inside one another:

```
<blockquote><blockquote><blockquote> Bob:
I was at the appointed place on time. When
you struck the match to light your cigar I
saw it was the face of the man wanted in
Chicago. Somehow I couldn't do it myself,
so I went around and got a plain clothes
man to do the
job.</blockquote></blockquote></blockquote
>
```

> Bob: I was at the appointed place on time. When you struck the match to light your cigar I saw it was the face of the man wanted in Chicago. Somehow I couldn't do it myself, so I went around and got a plain clothes man to do the job.

Because the amount of indentation is different in the two Kindle devices, the nesting on the two devices is also different. You can nest up to 3 levels (1 1/2 inches) on the Kindle 1 and up to 5 levels (1 3/8 inches) on the Kindle 2. After that, both Kindles give a partial indent to the next

<blockquote> and line up all subsequent <blockquote> indents with it.

Here is how nested block quotes show up on the Kindle 1 (Figure 5.3) and Kindle 2 (Figure 5.4):

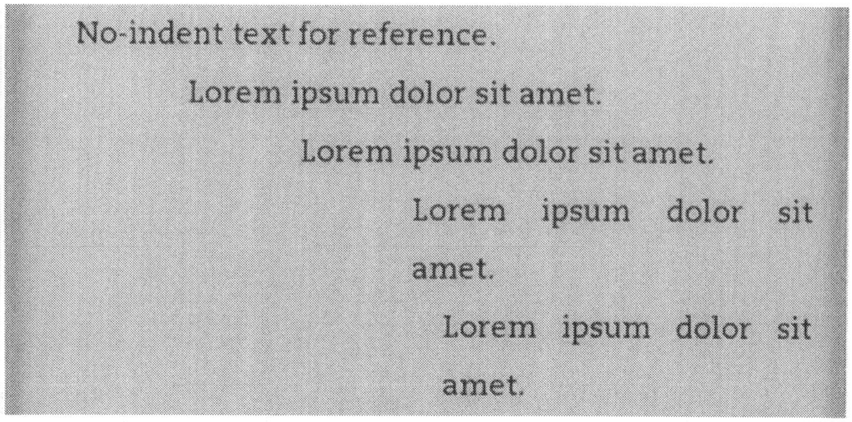

No-indent text for reference.

Lorem ipsum dolor sit amet.

Lorem ipsum dolor sit amet.

Lorem ipsum dolor sit amet.

Lorem ipsum dolor sit amet.

Figure 5.3

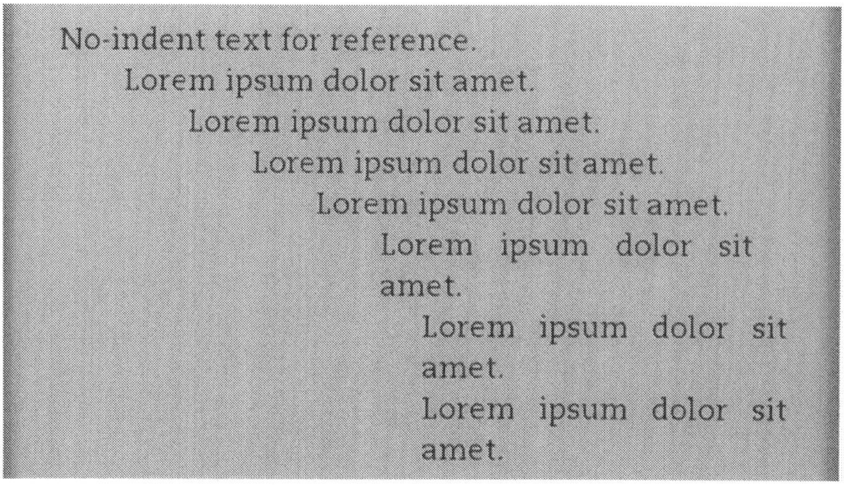

No-indent text for reference.

Lorem ipsum dolor sit amet.

Lorem ipsum dolor sit amet.

Lorem ipsum dolor sit amet.

Lorem ipsum dolor sit amet.

Lorem ipsum dolor sit amet.

Lorem ipsum dolor sit amet.

Lorem ipsum dolor sit amet.

Figure 5.4

Lists

There are two types of lists available in HTML: ordered and unordered. Ordered lists automatically place a number in front of each item, while unordered lists automatically place a bullet in front of each item. In most web browsers you can control the types of numbering and the symbols inserted, but the Kindle will only show numbers and bullets.

```
<ol>
  <li>apple</li>
  <ol>
    <li>orange</li>
    <ol>
      <li>grape</li>
    </ol>
  </ol>
</ol>
<ul>
  <li>apple</li>
  <ul>
    <li>orange</li>
    <ul>
      <li>grape</li>
    </ul>
  </ul>
</ul>
```

The text of the items in a list are indented the same amount as block quotes (0.5 inches on Kindle 1 and 0.25 inches on Kindle 2), but the number or bullet is placed to the left of that indent. You can nest lists within each other, but you run into the same issues with that process that you do with block quotes: the Kindle 1 will only really support three levels of indentation and the Kindle 2 will only support 5 levels, plus a lot of screen real estate is taken up with the white space on the left.

You can use the left-align style described on page 52 to force left-justification on your list elements.

It is also important to note that the size and placement of the bullets has changed on the Kindle 2.

There is an alternative to using traditional lists. You can use the same general markup described in the Poetry section on page 57 using hanging indents and non-breaking spaces to create lists that allow more indentation and the ability to change the number or bullet style. Here is an example of an outline created in this format:

```
<style type="text/css">
p.left {
   text-align: left;
}
</style>
. . . . . . . . . .
<p class="left" width="-
60">     V. 
 The Texas Revolution &mdash; October
2, 1835 through April 21, 1836</p>
<p class="left" width="-
90">     &n
bsp;   A.  The
Federal Rebellion Against Tyranny</p>
<p class="left" width="-
120">     &
nbsp;      &
nbsp; 1.  Organization of
Provisional Government</p>
<p class="left" width="-
120">      &
nbsp;      &
nbsp; 2.  The Siege of
Bexar</p>
<p class="left" width="-
120">      &
```

nbsp;   &
nbsp; 3. The Fall of the
Alamo</p>
<p class="left" width="-
90">   &n
bsp;   B. The
War of Independence</p>
<p class="left" width="-
120">   &
nbsp;   &
nbsp; 1. Convention of
1836</p>
<p class="left" width="-
120">   &
nbsp;   &
nbsp; 2. The Loss of South
Texas</p>
<p class="left" width="-
120">   &
nbsp;   &
nbsp; 3. Later Campaigns
and the Battle of San Jacinto</p>
<p class="left" width="-
60">   VI.
;The Republic of Texas — April 21,
1836 through December 29, 1845</p>
<p class="left" width="-
90">   &n
bsp;   A. Establ
ishment of Government</p>
<p class="left" width="-
120">   &
nbsp;   &
nbsp; 1. Problems of the
Government</p>

V. The Texas Revolution — October 2, 1835 through April 21, 1836

    A. The Federal Rebellion Against Tyranny

        1. Organization of Provisional Government

        2. The Siege of Bexar

        3. The Fall of the Alamo

    B. The War of Independence

        1. Convention of 1836

        2. The Loss of South Texas

        3. Later Campaigns and the Battle of San Jacinto

VI. The Republic of Texas — April 21, 1836 through December 29, 1845

    A. Establishment of Government

        1. Problems of the Government

There is no way to get the list items completely lined up at every font size. This will probably not matter much to your readers, though, as long as the indentation is consistent enough. Notice that the first line of the outline above (V. The Texas Revolution) uses the second poetry level indentation—a width of -60px and five non-breaking spaces. However, the next item at that same level (VI. The Republic of Texas) only uses four non-breaking spaces since the Roman numeral has an extra letter. You will have to tweak your outline like that to make sure everything is lined up as much as possible.

Also, notice that I have assigned the left-align style to the outline paragraphs. This ensures that when the text wraps it does not insert the extra spacing common with fully-justified text, which can make an outline like this harder to read.

Definition Lists

Definition lists are not used very often in HTML, but they are supported in the Kindle. A definition list actually consists of three separate tags. The `<dl>` tag is the surrounding tag. Inside that `<dl>` you can list a "definition term" in the `<dt>` tag and "definition data" in the `<dd>` tag. Without the `<dl>` tag, the other two tags will be ignored.

In the Kindle, Definition lists are indented the same way `<blockquote>` tags are. The only difference in formatting is that the contents of the `<dt>` tag are bolded.

You can create better formatting of lists like this using other styles mentioned here, so I do not suggest using definition lists unless you need to.

Headings

In HTML, headings are marked in tags like this:

```
<h1>Heading 1</h1>
<h2>Heading 2</h2>
<h3>Heading 3</h3>
<h4>Heading 4</h4>
<h5>Heading 5</h5>
<h6>Heading 6</h6>
```

Heading 1

Heading 2

Heading 3

Heading 4

Heading 5

Heading 6

Normal text

Each tag is supposed to format its contents progressively larger from `<h6>` up to `<h1>`. However, on the Kindle there is really not much of a difference between `<h6>` and `<h5>` at the medium font sizes. As the user adjusts the font size these headings also change. They generally stay in proportion to the regular paragraph font size, but in font size 4 `<h1>` reaches the maximum size allowed on the Kindle, in font size 5 `<h2>` reaches that maximum, and in font size 6 `<h3>` reaches that maximum. As you are planning your book layout you may want to keep these size differences in mind.

You can add the left-align, right-align, and centered styles to your headings.

Margins

In addition to the left margins we talked about in the Hanging Indent and Poetry sections above, the Kindle allows the creation of margins above and below headings, paragraphs, lists, and block quotes. Top margins can be added with the `height` attribute, but the Kindle also supports the use of the `margin-top` and `margin-bottom` CSS formatting.

The `height` attribute can be given a value in:

pixels (`height="40"`),
points (`height="40pt`),
percent (`height="10%"`),
or *em*-units (`height="2em"`).

Negative values are ignored.

The CSS `margin` commands can also use

pixels (`margin-top:40px;`),
points (`margin-top:40pt;`),
percent (`margin-top:10%;`),
and *em*-units (`margin-top:2em;`).

Note that the Kindle 1 (Figure 5.5) and Kindle 2 (Figure 5.6) will display the heights slightly differently due to differences in the default line heights assigned on the devices. Also, the size of the *em*-unit is different on the two devices. (Refer to the section about measurements on page 49 for more information about that.)

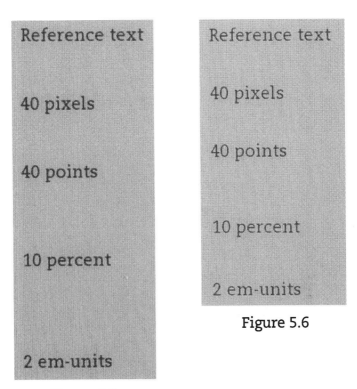

Figure 5.5

Figure 5.6

Margins are very useful when applied to headings, like this:

```
<h1 class="center" height="50">Man About
Town</h1>
<p class="center">by</p>
<h4 class="center">O. Henry</h4>
<p class="noind" height="30">There were
two or three things that I wanted to know.
I do not care about a mystery. So I began
to inquire.</p>
```

Kindle Formatting   Joshua Tallent

Man About Town

by

O. Henry

There were two or three things that I wanted to know. I do not care about a mystery. So I began to inquire.

Notice that I gave the `<h1>` a 50 pixel height and the first paragraph a 30 pixel height as well as a no-indent style. Formatting like that can effectively recreate the hard copy formatting at book chapter headings.

Margins also look very nice when applied to a book's subheadings. Adding a little 30 pixel height to them makes the text flow much better.

You can give block quotes and poetry a little more space with the `height` attribute. Just add a height (usually 20-30px is good) to the first `<blockquote>` or poetry tag and to the first paragraph following that text.

Tables

The Kindle 1 does not support HTML tables, but the Kindle 2 does. Table tags in your HTML file on a Kindle 1 (Figure 5.7) will be completely ignored, and the resulting content will be pretty much un-readable. On the Kindle 2 (Figure 5.8), the table tags will be interpreted properly, and the resulting table will be displayed on the screen. If the table is wider than the screen allows, the user can click the joystick right and left while selecting the table to scroll it horizontally.

Quarters

Revenues Quarters Revenues

Q1 02 $1,556,499 Q3 05 $2,310,291

Q2 02 $1,258,989 Q4 05 $2,175,131

Q3 02 $1,329,548 Q1 06 $4,100,000

Q4 02 $1,649,144 Q2 06 $4,000,000

Q1 03 $1,794,544 Q3 06 $4,900,000

Q2 03 $1,842,502 Q4 06 $7,000,000

Q3 03 $1,789,455 Q1 07 $7,500,000

Q4 03 $1,917,384 Q2 07 $8,100,000

Q1 04 $1,794,130 Q3 07 $8,000,000

Q2 04 $1,887,900 Q4 07 $8,200,000

Q3 04 $2,460,343 Q1 08 $10,100,000

Q4 04 $3,477,130 Q2 08 $11,600,000

Q1 05 $3,161,049 Q3 08 $13,900,000

Q2 05 $3,182,499 Q4 08 $16,800,000

Figure
5.7

Quarters	Revenues	Quarters	Revenues
Q1 02	$1,556,499	Q3 05	$2,310,291
Q2 02	$1,258,989	Q4 05	$2,175,131
Q3 02	$1,329,548	Q1 06	$4,100,000
Q4 02	$1,649,144	Q2 06	$4,000,000
Q1 03	$1,794,544	Q3 06	$4,900,000
Q2 03	$1,842,502	Q4 06	$7,000,000
Q3 03	$1,789,455	Q1 07	$7,500,000
Q4 03	$1,917,384	Q2 07	$8,100,000
Q1 04	$1,794,130	Q3 07	$8,000,000
Q2 04	$1,887,900	Q4 07	$8,200,000
Q3 04	$2,460,343	Q1 08	$10,100,000
Q4 04	$3,477,130	Q2 08	$11,600,000
Q1 05	$3,161,049	Q3 08	$13,900,000
Q2 05	$3,182,499	Q4 08	$16,800,000

Figure
5.8

However, because the Kindle 1 does not support tables, I do not suggest that you start using the table tags just yet. There are still a lot of Kindle 1 users out there, and using HTML tables in your books will leave them wondering what the mess of words on their screen is supposed to be.

So, there are two useable ways to handle table content. In many books tables are used to create formatting, not really to show tabular data. For instance, a list might be placed in a table to reduce the amount of the page it consumes. In instances like that, it is best to make the list into a regular list.

There are other times when the table data can be constructed as text in a way that makes sense to the user. For instance, this table of eBook Revenues from the IDPF:

Quarters	Revenues
Q1 07	$7,500,000
Q2 07	$8,100,000
Q3 07	$8,000,000
Q4 07	$8,200,000
Q1 08	$10,100,000
Q2 08	$11,600,000

can be formatted like this in the Kindle:

```
<p class="noind"
height="20"><b>Quarter:</b> Q1 07</p>
<p class="noind"><b>Revenues:</b>
$7,500,000</p>
<p class="noind"
height="20"><b>Quarter:</b> Q2 07</p>
<p class="noind"><b>Revenues:</b>
$8,100,000</p>
<p class="noind"
height="20"><b>Quarter:</b> Q3 07</p>
<p class="noind"><b>Revenues:</b>
$8,000,000</p>
<p class="noind"
height="20"><b>Quarter:</b> Q4 07</p>
<p class="noind"><b>Revenues:</b>
$8,200,000</p>
```

```
<p class="noind"
height="20"><b>Quarter:</b> Q1 08</p>
<p class="noind"><b>Revenues:</b>
$10,100,000</p>
<p class="noind"
height="20"><b>Quarter:</b> Q2 08</p>
<p class="noind"><b>Revenues:</b>
$11,600,000</p>
```

Notice that the table headers were repeated for each row of data, and that the "Quarter" paragraphs have a top margin. This results in a very readable set of data that is easy to format.

The other option for including tabular data in your book is to convert it into an image (usually by taking a screen shot with your image creation program). This option works well for smaller tables that really need to be in a tabular format. However, if you are planning to make a large table into an image, you will probably need to break it up into several pieces so that the text stays readable, and you may even want to turn the images 90° counterclockwise to take full advantage of the screen size.

Quarter: Q1 07

Revenues: $7,500,000

Quarter: Q2 07

Revenues: $8,100,000

Quarter: Q3 07

Revenues: $8,000,000

Quarter: Q4 07

Revenues: $8,200,000

Quarter: Q1 08

Revenues: $10,100,000

Quarter: Q2 08

Revenues: $11,600,000

Borders

Borders are not supported on the Kindle 1, but you can, as you see above, add borders around tables in the Kindle 2. As a matter of fact, you can even use the `background-color` CSS property to assign a grayscale color in a table cell. See the section about Pull Quotes and Sidebars on page 110 for an example of this formatting and an explanation of its pros and cons. Borders are not supported around other tags on the Kindle 2. To set apart text in a way that is supported on both devices, use the <hr/> (Horizontal Rule) tag described on page 91.

Images

The Kindle screen is an E Ink Vizplex electronic paper display (EPD). The Kindle 1 screen supports four grayscale levels (black, white, 33% gray, and 66% gray), and the Kindle 2 screen supports 16 grayscale levels. Both screens handle a variety of image types remarkably well. I have formatted books for my clients with charts and graphs, company logos, maps, and photos of people and places. These all display okay on the Kindle 1, but are much better on the Kindle 2.

Dimensions

There has been a lot of talk on the Kindle DTP forums about what dimensions an image should be to take full advantage of the available screen real estate. The consensus opinion, and the response stated by the DTP admin, has been that 450 pixels wide by 550 pixels high (a ratio of 9:11) is the proper scale. In the course of my formatting work and testing I have found that there is a little bit more to the story than that.

The actual size of the viewable book area on the Kindle 1 screen is 524px × 640px, and the viewable book area on the Kindle 2 screen is 520px × 622px. Any images larger or smaller than that (including those sized 450px × 550px) will be automatically re-sized until the width or height fits the viewable book area. At 261px × 319px on Kindle 1 and 260px × 311px on Kindle 2 (half the size of the viewable book area) the image is no longer resized to fit the book area's width or height. This is important when you are creating logos or other small images for your book. Logos usually look great when sized around 75–100px wide. However, images will still lose some quality when reduced in size, especially photos. I suggest that you keep your images at the Kindle 2 dimensions (520px × 622px) if you can, so that your image quality does not suffer.

In case you are wondering, I found these numbers using an old trick that photographers use when testing a camera lens. My brother, a semi-professional photographer, was instrumental in this testing. We created an image with 1 pixel lines alternating black and white, both horizontal and vertical. Then, we tested that image at various sizes on the Kindle. When an image is being re-sized by the device the lines show up on the screen with some distortion. When the image is not being re-sized the lines show up clearly defined.

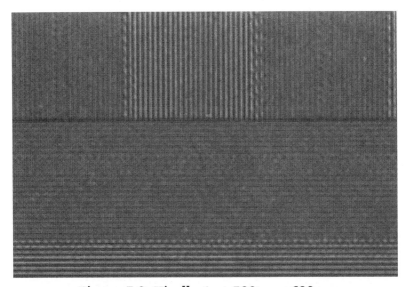

Figure 5.9: Kindle 1 at 520px × 622px

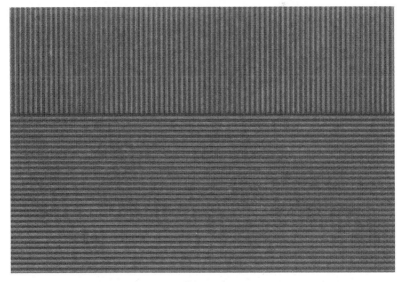

Figure 5.10: Kindle 1 at 524px × 640px

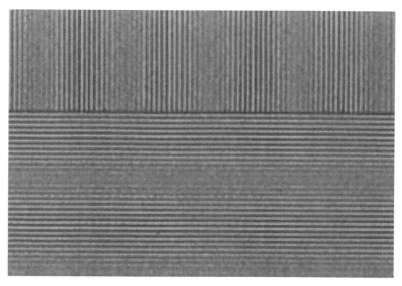

Figure 5.11: Kindle 2 at 524px × 640px

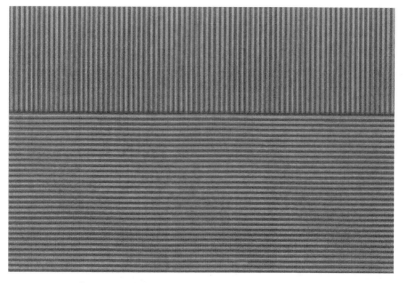

Figure 5.12: Kindle 2 at 520px × 622px

If your image has captions, you will need to either add the caption text to the image itself, or size the image at dimensions that will allow the text to be seen underneath it. The benefit of adding the caption to the image is that you don't have to worry about the image and caption showing up on different screens ("pages"). The benefit of using text under the image is that it can be re-sized by the reader. Whichever way you decide to go, you will usually need about 30-50 pixels of space to write your caption. Don't forget, though, that the caption font size will change with the rest of the text, and you will not be able to control whether or not that forces some of the caption text to the next screen.

Colors

While the Kindle screen is not color, highly suggest that you keep your images in color for two reasons. First, at some point (probably in 2011) the E Ink Corporation will begin mass-producing a color electronic paper screen, so there is a decent possibility that a later version of the Kindle will support color. It would be best for authors and publishers to plan for this so that they do not have to re-upload their books with color images. Second, many Mobipocket-supported devices and the iPhone support color images. Since Kindle books are now available on the iPhone, and since you might want to sell your book in the Mobipocket format, leaving the images in color is a good idea.

Resolution

The Kindle screen supports up to 167 pixels per inch (ppi), so it is best to work with images in that resolution or better if possible. Print images are usually at least 300ppi, and Internet images are usually 72ppi. Both will usually work fine for the Kindle, though the 72ppi images might be a little bit more grainy.

File Type

The Kindle supports PNG, JPG, GIF, and BMP files. The file type you choose for your images will probably depend on what format they are in already. PNGs are usually very good for charts, graphs, and other images with text; JPGs are commonly used for photographs; GIFs can be used with charts and graphs, or to keep your file size down if you have a lot of images; I don't suggest using BMPs since the other formats are usually better. Note that although Amazon requires a TIFF or JPG file for the book cover image on the DTP, the Kindle itself does not support the TIFF format. If you are going to include the cover image at the front of your book, you will need to convert it into the JPG format.

File Size

Image file size is affected by most of the factors above. The biggest influence is the dimensions of the image, but color, resolution, and even file type are also contributors. If your book has a lot of images, you may want to play with these variables to reduce the image sizes. The DTP admin has stated that images larger than 64 kilobytes will be automatically reduced, but I have not been able to confirm that statement in my testing. Needless to say, your readers will not want to take up the majority of their memory with one book, so do take the image file size into consideration when preparing for publication.

Rotation

Most images will look fine on the Kindle just as they are, but there are times when rotating an image 90° is actually preferable, such as when you have a graph or chart that requires more width to be readable. If you do rotate an image, be sure to rotate it counterclockwise. The most natural way for most users to turn the device is clockwise, so rotating your image the opposite direction will make it show up properly. An example of this rotation can be seen in the chart on page 79.

Handling Different Kinds of Images

Following are some samples of how different kinds of images look on the Kindle. For a few of them I have included photos of both the Kindle 1 and Kindle 2 so you can see how the 16-level grayscale screen on the Kindle 2 affects some images.

Chart

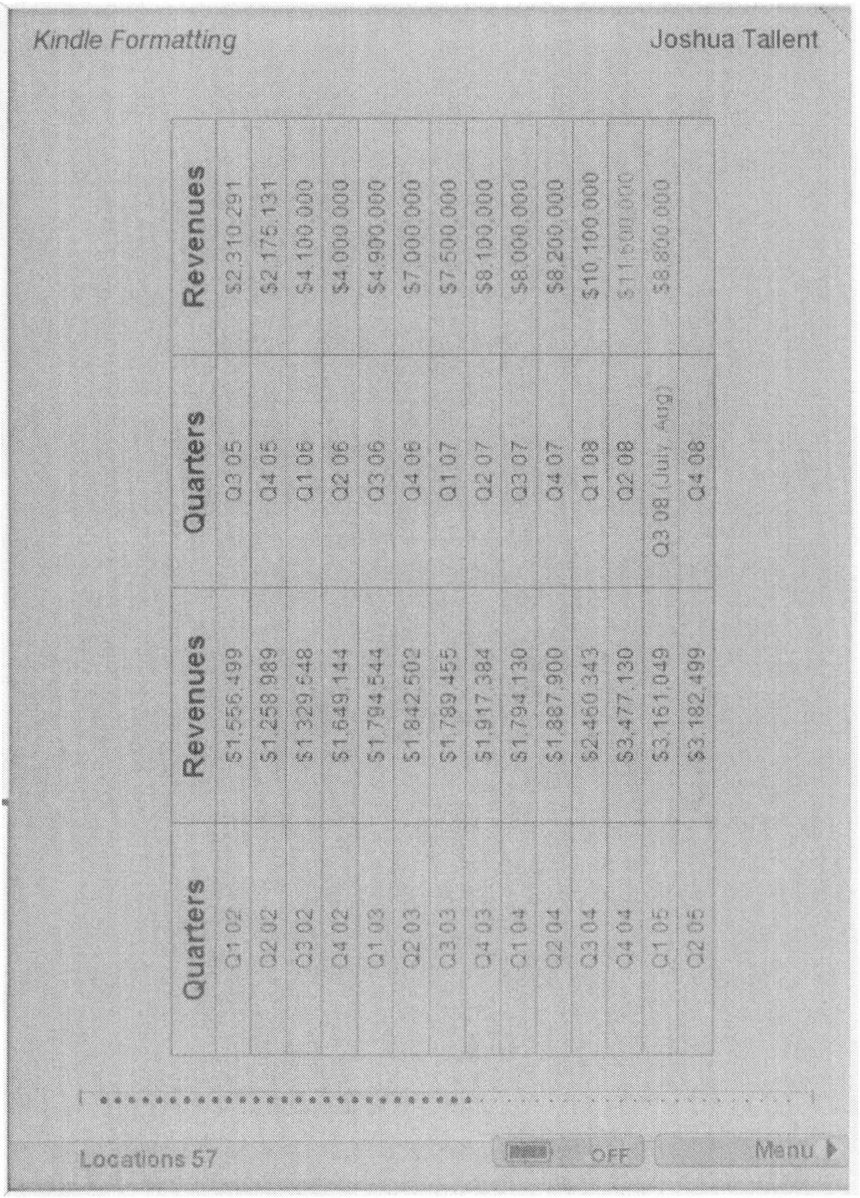

Figure 5.13: Chart on the Kindle 1.

Graph

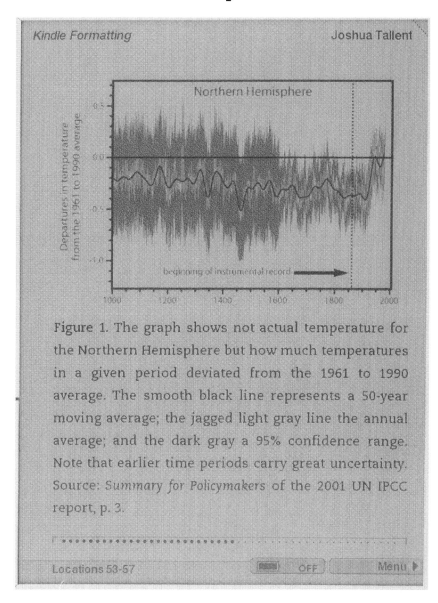

Kindle Formatting   Joshua Tallent

Figure 1. The graph shows not actual temperature for the Northern Hemisphere but how much temperatures in a given period deviated from the 1961 to 1990 average. The smooth black line represents a 50-year moving average; the jagged light gray line the annual average; and the dark gray a 95% confidence range. Note that earlier time periods carry great uncertainty. Source: *Summary for Policymakers* of the 2001 UN IPCC report, p. 3.

Locations 53-57   OFF   Menu ▶

Figure 5.14: Graph on the Kindle 1.

The Deniers by Lawrence Solomon. Image Courtesy of Richard Vigilante Books, http://richardvigilantebooks.com.

Graph

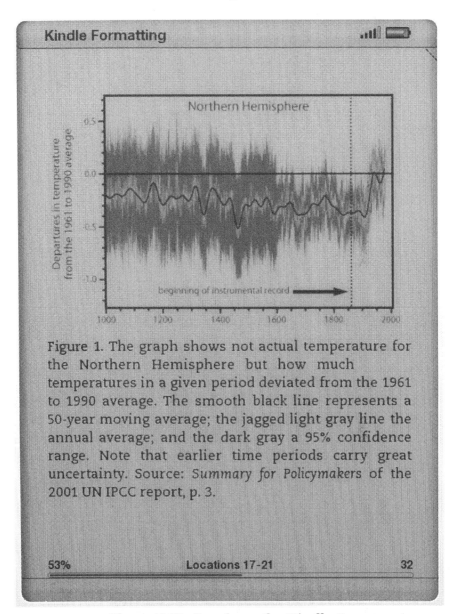

Figure 5.15: Graph on the Kindle 2.

The Deniers by Lawrence Solomon. Image Courtesy of Richard Vigilante Books, http://richardvigilantebooks.com.

Map

Figure 5.16: Map on the Kindle 1.

The Rand McNally Road Atlas of Washington State. Image Courtesy of Rand McNally, http://randmcnally.com.

Map

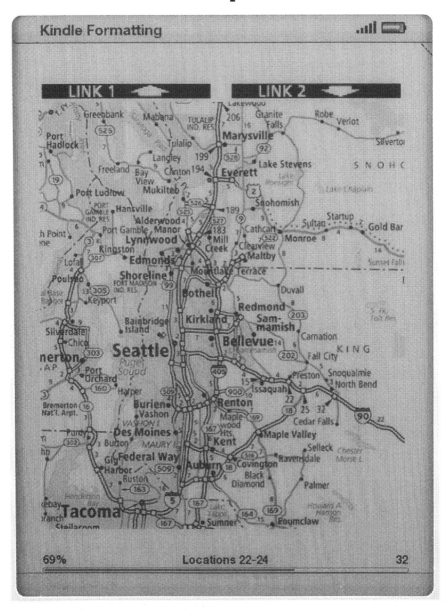

Figure 5.17: Map on the Kindle 2.

The Rand McNally Road Atlas of Washington State. Image Courtesy of Rand McNally, http://randmcnally.com.

Person

Figure 5.18: Photo of a person on the Kindle 1.

Person

Figure 5.19: Photo of a person on the Kindle 2.

Landscape

Figure 5.20: Photo of a landscape on the Kindle 1.
Forsand, Norway.

Landscape

Figure 5.21: Photo of a landscape on the Kindle 2.
Forsand, Norway.

Inserting Images

When your images are ready to go, you will need to create <img> tags for them in your HTML. Inside that tag you will need to include the src and alt attributes. The src attribute contains the path to your image (the "source"). All of your images must be in the same directory as your HTML file, not in a subdirectory or somewhere else. Also, the Kindle does not allow images in books to be loaded from the Internet, even if Whispernet is turned on. The alt (alternate text) attribute contains a description of the image. The alt description is not actually required by the Kindle, but it is a good coding practice to include it.

I suggest that you place large images in a centered paragraph that has had the first-line indent removed. For example:

```
<style type="text/css">
p.center {
  text-indent: 0;
  text-align: center;
}
</style>
..........
<p class="center"><img src="image01.png"
alt="House in Norway" /></p>
```

Notice that the image tag has a closing forward slash at the end of it. This is used because, unlike most other tags, the image tag does not have a closing tag. It is a good coding practice to close your tags, and the "/" gives you that ability.

If you add a caption below your image, you can also center it and add other effects like <b>, <i>, and <small>.

```
<p class="center"><small><b>Forsand,
Norway is a beautiful vacation
spot.</b></small></p>
```

Inserting images within the text of a paragraph is also possible. This is especially useful when you are inserting symbols that are not supported on the Kindle, such as math functions. For example:

```
<p>Here, <img src="math1.png"
alt="binomial coefficient" align="middle"
/> is the binomial coefficient</p>
```

Here, $\binom{n}{k}$ is the binomial coefficient

The `align` attribute in that `<img>` tag gives the image a vertical alignment in relation to the surrounding text. The values that you can use in that attribute include:

`top`	Aligns the top of the image with the top of the current line.
`middle`	Centers the image vertically in the current line
`bottom`	Aligns the bottom of the image with the bottom of the current line

The default setting is `bottom`.

Anchor Tags

Anchor tags are used in HTML to create web and bookmark hyperlinks, and to mark bookmark anchors in the HTML file that can be linked to. You can create links to web pages in your Kindle book, and users who have Whispernet turned on will be taken to those web pages in the "Experimental" browser when they click on the links. For example:

```
<a href="http://kindleformatting.com">
Kindle Formatting</a>
```

This feature opens up virtually endless possibilities. For instance, you could create a page with more information about the book on your website that the reader can easily visit. You could also create a survey on your website that the reader can fill out and submit directly from their Kindle in the web browser. Because the Kindle reads unencrypted Mobipocket books, you could even add links to samples of other books in Mobipocket format on your website, and readers can download those samples directly to their device.

Special Links

Speaking of samples, Amazon automatically generates a sample consisting of the first 10 percent of the book for all books uploaded through the DTP. These samples all have two unique links on their last page: one to the book's product page and one to buy the book with one click. The product page that is shown with the first link is not the one you would see in the "Experimental" Web browser if you just went to the Amazon website. It is the same product page layout you see when you are browsing the Kindle Store on the device, which is much nicer and has easy-to-use buttons for purchasing the book directly from the Kindle.

Well, you can use these links in your book, as well. For instance, you can create a listing of your other books that are for sale on the Kindle Store, with links to their product pages and links that allow users to buy the other books with one click.

These links both require the Amazon ASIN for the Kindle book you are pointing to, which you can find on the book's regular product page in the Product Details section. The links will not work properly for other items in the Amazon store.

Product page link:

> https://www.amazon.com/gp/g7g/fws/anchor/detailPageEbook.xml?asin=xxxxxxxxxx

Buy Now link:

> https://www.amazon.com/gp/g7g/fws/anchor/buyEbook.xml?asin= xxxxxxxxxx

Bookmark Links

Bookmarks can be defined in your book using the `name` attribute. For instance, you can mark all of your chapters with an anchor tag to make links in your Table of Contents.

```
<a name="chap1"/><h1>Chapter 1</h1>
```

To link to this anchor in your Table of Contents, just use a bookmark reference in the anchor tag by adding a hash symbol in front of the name you are linking to:

```
<p class="noind"><a href="#chap1">Chapter
1</a></p>
```

We will cover TOC mark-up in more detail on page 104.

When you add named anchors within your book, it is a best practice to place them before any paragraph or heading tags, not after them. If you place them in after the tag, it is possible that the user will not see the formatting when the Kindle loads the content on the screen.

Horizontal Rules

While borders are not supported on the Kindle 1 and are only supported around tables on the Kindle 2, you can add a horizontal line in your text to break up the content using the `<hr/>` tag. I have used these in previous projects to indicate sidebars, to indicate a scene change in the text, and to bookend pull quotes. We will cover sidebar and pull quote markup with some examples on page 110.

The Kindle formats the default horizontal rule as a gray line about 2 pixels high extending across almost the entire width of the viewable book area. You can assign a width of your own to the `<hr/>` tag using the `width` attribute. As in other places, the `width` attribute will accept units in pixels (`width="100"`), percent (`width="50%"`), *em*-units (`width="30em"`), or points (`width="70pt"`). The default display can be duplicated at a width of 475px, and you can extend the line to the edges of the book display area with a `width="500"`. This is somewhat confusing when you consider the Kindle's screen resolution and viewable book area (see page 74), but I have been unable to figure out the reason for this discrepancy.

You can also assign a height (top margin) to your `<hr/>` tag, as described in the section on margins on page 68. Unfortunately, there is no way to make a `<hr/>` display flush left, but you can simulate a flush right style by placing the `<hr/>` inside one or more `<blockquote>` tags. Examples of this can be seen on page 110.

Unfortunately, the shading and vertical size of the `<hr />` tag cannot be adjusted.

Comments

Many times it is helpful to place a comment in your HTML code so that anyone looking at the code later will have a description of what you were doing. They can also be useful for labeling parts of the book in your code or marking places you need to remember to work on as you are formatting your file. Comments in HTML are placed in a special tag like this:

```
<!-- I am a comment -->
```

These are never seen by the reader, and should only be used to make behind the scenes notes in the code.

Page Breaks

There are times when you will want to force some content to start on a new screen ("page") in your book. These page breaks are not hard to format, but they require a special tag that is not actually HTML: `<mbp:pagebreak />`. The "mbp" actually stands for "Mobipocket," since the Kindle eBook format is based on the Mobipocket eBook format. You should place one of these page break tags in front of each chapter in your book, and possibly in front of other items, like images, which may need to be forced to the next page.

```
<mbp:pagebreak />
<h1>Chapter 1</h1>
. . . . . . . . . .
<mbp:pagebreak />
<p class="center"><img src="image01.png"
alt="House in Norway" /></p>
<p class="caption"><small><b>Forsand,
Norway is a beautiful vacation
spot.</b></small></p>
```

Microsoft Word inserts a page break like this:

```
<br clear=all style='page-break-before:
always'>
```

The effectiveness of that tag is not guaranteed, however, so I suggest you replace it with the `<mbp:pagebreak />` tag.

Special Characters and Inserting Symbols

The Kindle format supports a wide variety of Unicode characters, including most Latin characters, (Basic Latin; Latin-1; Latin Extended A and B; and Latin Extended Additional); all of the Greek characters and pre-composed Greek characters with diacriticals (Greek and Greek Extended); a variety of mathematical symbols; as well as some arrows, musical notations, and Dingbat symbols. A complete list of the supported character sets can be found on page 155.

To ensure that these characters display properly, you will need to convert them into HTML entities. An entity is a code that tells the Kindle what character to display in the text. Entities all start with an ampersand (&) and end with a semicolon (;). The interior text can be a name (é), a decimal number (é) or a hexadecimal number (é), but the name is usually easiest to remember. For instance, if you have the word "résumé" in your book, it can be coded like this in the HTML:

```
r&eacute;sum&eacute;
```

résumé

I have included a chart in Appendix C that gives you the valid codes for many of the common characters in the Latin-1 character set. In the Book Tools download section of my website I have included a printable list of all of the characters in the entire Latin range, the Greek and Greek pre-composed characters, and a selection of other common symbols that are supported on the Kindle. In that download you will also find a Perl script that you can run on your HTML file to convert the common Latin-1 characters into entities automatically.

To find the characters in the Latin-1 character set manually in Windows, you can do a search in your HTML document using this Regular Expression:

[€-ÿ]

(Note: Due to a bug, this does not work in Notepad++ yet.) Those are the first (€) and last (ÿ) characters in the Latin-1 character range. To type those characters into the find box in your HTML editor program, hold down the Alt key on your keyboard and type the 4-digit number for the character using the number pad on your keyboard (not the numbers above the main keys): 0128 and 0255. Alternatively, you can use the Character Map utility that comes with Windows to copy these characters. That can be found in the Start Menu, under Programs, Accessories.

Macintosh users have similar options for inserting Latin-1 characters, and OS X comes with a built-in character map of its own. However, you may find that characters 0128 and 0255 on your Mac do not look the same as what you see printed here.

If you insert any special characters into your book, it is best to make the encoding of the file UTF-8, not ASCII. This is usually an option in the Save As menu of your text editor. Also, to ensure the Kindle properly formats the entities, be sure to but the UTF-8 meta tag at the top of your HTML:

```
<meta http-equiv="Content-Type"
content="text/html; charset=UTF-8" />
```

Foreign Languages

The Kindle supports the use of Greek text, including the full range of pre-composed characters with diacritics, but it does not support any other non-Latin foreign language characters.

Caseins are a family of phosphoproteins (αS1, αS2, β, κ) that account for nearly 80% of bovine milk proteins.

To insert other languages in your text, you will need to use images. A height of 14-16 pixels is usually good when you are taking screen shots or creating images of text. See the images section on page 89 for information on formatting inline images.

Non-breaking Spaces

During conversion to HTML, Microsoft Word inserts some non-breaking spaces (, , U+00A0;) where there are tabs in the original file. It will also sometimes place a non-breaking space and a regular space between sentences. While sometimes these non-breaking spaces do not actually cause problems, they can become problematic when they have been placed at the beginning of a paragraph to create indentation. For example:

```
<p>There were two or three things that I
wanted to know. I do not care about a
mystery. So I began to inquire.</p>
<p>      &nb
sp;     It took me two
weeks to find out what women carry in
dress suit cases. And then I began to ask
why a mattress is made in two
pieces....</p>
```

> There were two or three things that I wanted to know. I do not care about a mystery. So I began to inquire.
>
> It took me two weeks to find out what women carry in dress suit cases. And then I began to ask why a mattress is made in two pieces....

In general, it is best to remove the non-breaking spaces that Word inserts. I usually change all of the non-breaking spaces in a Kindle HTML file into regular spaces, and then do a search to find all of the places where two or more spaces occur. That allows me to fix any weird formatting problems, of which these extra spaces are usually a symptom.

Hyphenated Words

You are likely to find a character known as a soft hyphen (`&shy;`, `&#173;`, `U+00AD`) at various places throughout your book. Publishers and book layout tools commonly add this character inside long words at syllable breaks to allow the word to break into two parts at the end of a line. In print books, this makes full justification much nicer because the flow of the text is not interrupted by large amounts of space on a line left by a long word wrapping to the next line. The Kindle does not support the soft-hyphen character; it actually displays it in the text, regardless of whether or not the word is breaking across a line break. You will need to remove all of these characters from your book.

However, be careful when removing them because sometimes the soft hyphens are actually in places where a regular hyphen should be, such as between compound words with three or more pieces.

Special Combination Letters

In some books, especially those that start out as PDF files from a publisher, you will find that some combinations of letters have been replaced with entities for combined letters called ligatures. The most common of these ligatures are:

`&#64256;`	ff
`&#64257;`	fi
`&#64258;`	fl
`&#64259;`	ffi
`&#64260;`	ffl

These are inserted by some publishers to ensure proper display and printing of the character combinations in the font chosen for the print book. Replacing them can be a small chore, especially since the conversion process may add a space after the entity when there should not be one. So, the word "find" may look like "`&#64257;` nd". The replacement process can be automated a little bit by doing a find and replace on the most unique words in the book, and by using this regex, switching out the entity as needed:

Find: `([a-z])(&#64256;)([a-z])`

Replace: `\1ff\2`

Other than that, you will just have to take some time to look at all of these instances and determine if the space after the entity is needed or not.

Conclusion

The formatting information in this chapter will be some of the most important information you have available as you convert your book. Be sure to refer to the sections above as often as necessary. In the next chapter we will look at some real-world examples of eBook formatting.

Chapter 6

Formatting Examples

In this chapter I will give you some examples of formatting you might use in certain sections of your book. These examples are provided merely as a guide to formatting, not as a hard-and-fast rule for how the pages in question should look.

Title Page

Most books have a couple of key elements on the title page: book title, subtitle, the word "by", author's name, publisher's logo, and publisher's location information. You could format those elements like this:

```
<h1 class="center" height="50">Man About
Town</h1>
<p class="center" height="30">by</p>
<h3 class="center" height="20">O.
Henry</h3>
<p class="center" height="50"><img
src="logo.png" alt="Vintage Volumes"
/></p>
<p class="center"><b>Austin, Texas</b></p>
```

Of course, there are always other ways to create a Title page, and some have much more information than the simple example above.

Copyright Page

The copyright page in most books contains a large amount of data about the book and its publication.

```
<mbp:pagebreak />
<p class="noind"><small><b>The Four
Million</b></small></p>
<p class="noind"><small>Copyright &copy;
1906 O. Henry. All rights reserved. No
part of this book may be reproduced or
retransmitted in any form or by any means
without the written permission of the
publisher.</small></p>
<p class="noind"
height="20"><small>Published by Vintage
Volumes&trade;</small></p>
<p class="noind"><small>Austin, Texas
U.S.A.</small></p>
<p
class="noind"><small>www.example.com</smal
l></p>
<p class="center"
height="20"><small><b>Publisher&rsquo;s
Cataloging-in-Publication</b></small></p>
<p class="noind" height="20"><small>Henry,
O.</small></p>
<blockquote><small>The four million / by
O. Henry.</small></blockquote>
<blockquote><small>p.
cm.</small></blockquote>
<blockquote><small>&ldquo;Thought-
provoking short storied from the master of
the surprise
ending.&rdquo;</small></blockquote>
<blockquote><small>LCCN:
6516516584</small></blockquote>
<blockquote><small>ISBN: 978-0-12345-678-9
(paperback)</small></blockquote>
<blockquote><small>ISBN: 978-1-98765-432-1
(hardcover)</small></blockquote>
```

```
<blockquote height="20"><small>1. Short
Stories--Classic.</small></blockquote>
<p class="noind"><small>2. Short Stories--
20th Century. I.
Title.</small></blockquote>
<p class="noind"
height="20"><small>UA65.R68Q68
2008      &n
bsp; 485&rsquo;.325&rsquo;1588</small
></p>
<p width="90"><small>QVI08-
700583</small></p>
```

As you can see, I usually try to match the indentation formatting in the Library of Congress section. In this case, I used <blockquote> tags, but you can also use the poetry mark-up shown on page 57.

The Four Million

Copyright © 1906 O. Henry. All rights reserved. No part of this book may be reproduced or retransmitted in any form or by any means without the written permission of the publisher.

Publisher's Cataloging-in-Publication

Henry, O.

The four million / by O. Henry.

p. cm.

"Thought-provoking short storied from the master of the surprise ending."

LCCN: 6516516584

ISBN: 978-0-12345-678-9 (paperback)

ISBN: 978-1-98765-432-1 (hardcover)

1. Short Stories--Classic.

2. Short Stories--20th Century. I. Title.

UA65.R68Q68 2008　　　485'.325'1588

QVI08-700583

Locations 70-78　　　　　　　　OFF　　　　Menu ▶

Table of Contents

The Table of Contents (TOC) is one of the most important parts of your book. A common complaint about eBooks compared to their print counterparts is the inability for the reader to easily see where they are in the book or to navigate between sections. The TOC alleviates that issue. It also allows your readers to easily skip forward or backward in the book and to find sections that they might otherwise overlook altogether, such as a glossary or an index.

Page numbers in an eBook can be useful or irrelevant. They are useful if the book is used for reference and will be cited in a paper or another book, but even in those cases writing style guides give ways to cite a source when the page numbers are not available. On the Kindle, the text will re-flow when the reader changes the font size, so what they see on the screen is not equivalent to what is on a page in the print book.

As a result, the page numbers listed in your Table of Contents will be irrelevant to the reader. They can be left in, but in most cases they will just be a distraction. The same is not true of page numbers in a subject index, as we will discuss below.

To make the TOC in your book useful to the reader, each item should be linked to its position in the book. This goes for all chapter titles, any major subtitles you feel are important, the bibliography, index, about the author, and glossary sections—basically, anything you want the reader to see. That means your TOC may look a little bit different than the one in the print book.

Also, while it is helpful to have some subheadings listed in your TOC, you should be careful not to put in too many. Some readers may be turned off by the apparent size of the book if every single subheading level is included in the TOC. Usually one level is enough.

To create the links in your TOC, use the bookmark anchors described on page 90. For example:

```
<style type="text/css">
p.left {
    text-align: left;
}
</style>
. . . . . . . . .
<a name="TOC"/><h2>Contents</h2>
<p width="-30" class="left"><a
href="#acknow">Acknowledgements</a></p>
<p width="-30" class="left"><a
href="#preface">Preface</a></p>
<p width="-30" class="left"><a
href="#start">Introduction</a></p>
<p width="-30" class="left"><a
href="#chap1">Chapter 1</a></p>
<p width="-30" class="left"><a
href="#chap2">Chapter 2</a></p>
    <blockquote class="left"><a
    href="#sect1">Section
    1</a></blockquote>
    <blockquote class="left"><a
    href="#sect2">Section
    2</a></blockquote>
    <blockquote class="left"><a
    href="#sect3">Section
    3</a></blockquote>
<p width="-30" class="left"><a
href="#chap3">Chapter 3</a></p>
<p width="-30" class="left"><a
href="#chap4">Chapter 4</a></p>
<p width="-30" class="left"><a
href="#biblio">Bibliography</a></p>
<p width="-30" class="left"><a
href="#index">Index</a></p>
<p width="-30" class="left"><a
href="#author">About the Author</a></p>
```

There are a few important elements to point out in this example. First, there is a named anchor in front of the <h2> heading, like this: <a name="TOC"/>. This anchor is required by the Kindle in order for the link to the Table of Contents in the Kindle book menu to be activated.

Second, the link to the Introduction is `<a href="#start">`. This is another named anchor required by the Kindle. It determines where the book opens to for the first time after the user buys it and where the "Go to Beginning" link in the Kindle book menu sends the reader. This anchor can be placed anywhere, but the most common place to put it is at the introduction or the first chapter.

We will talk more about these two links and more in the section about creating the Guide in a Mobipocket book on page 123.

Third, the paragraphs are given a hanging left indent (`width="-30"`) and are left aligned (`class="left"`). This is very useful in the Table of Contents because it makes the lines wrap nicely when they are long or when the font size is large, but removes the extra spacing that is inserted when fully-justified lines wrap.

Fourth, I used the `<blockquote>` tag for the subheadings under Chapter 2. While it would be great to have the option of using a poetry-style paragraph tag (described on page 57) the non-breaking spaces at the beginning of the paragraph would cause the Kindle 1 to treat the paragraph as if it includes un-linked text. So, instead of immediately taking the reader to the subheading (the default action when a paragraph only consists of a link), they would first see a pop-up menu and would be required to select the link from there. This is not a problem in the Kindle 2, of course, since it uses the 5-way joystick for navigation.

Kindle Formatting   Joshua Tallent

Contents

Locations 78-85   OFF   Menu ▶

Headings

Closely related to the Table of Contents are the book's headings and subheadings. There are a variety of ways to format the headings in your books, so let's look at a few examples. If you want a simple chapter heading, you can do something like this:

```
<style type="text/css">
    h2 {text-align: center;}
    p.noind {text-indent: 0;}
</style>
.........
<mbp:pagebreak />
<a name="#chap1"></a><h2
height="30">Chapter 1</h2>
<p class="noind" height="30">The year 1866
was signalised by a remarkable
incident...</p>
```

Chapter 1

The year 1866 was signalised by a remarkable incident...

The heading is centered and given a top margin of 30 pixels, and the first paragraph is given a no-indent style with a top margin of its own. You could also give the paragraph a more pronounced top margin, a style that is common in some print books. Notice that the anchor tag is in front of the <h2> tag. As mentioned above, placing the anchor there will mitigate problems with the style of the heading being lost when the user follows the link from the Table of Contents.

Another example:

```
<style type="text/css">
    h2 {text-align: center;}
    h3 {text-align: center;}
    p.noind {text-indent: 0;}
</style>
. . . . . . . . . .
<mbp:pagebreak />
<a name="#chap1"></a><h3
height="30">1</h3>
<h2>A Shifting Reef</h2>
<p class="noind" height="30">The year 1866
was signalised by a remarkable
incident...</p>
```

In this example, the chapter number is placed in an `<h3>` tag, and the chapter name is placed in an `<h2>`. This formatting imitates another layout commonly found in print books.

The possibilities here are practically endless, so it should be fairly easy to mimic whatever style is used in your print book.

Subheadings

If your book has multiple levels of subheadings, it is important to clearly identify the heading structure through unique formatting so that your readers can follow the flow of your content easily. As I mentioned in the section on headings on page 67, the `<h5>` and `<h6>` headings are not really that different in the Kindle, so you essentially have 5 levels of formatting to work with. You can increase the number of available levels by adding italics and all-caps formatting, and by changing the alignment of the headings.

Also, it is important to add a top margin to your subheadings. Usually 20px or 30px is sufficient, but headings with no top margin can get lost in the text of your book.

Pull Quotes and Sidebars

Since the Kindle does not support floating elements, the placement and formatting of pull quotes and sidebars becomes a little bit tricky. The first issue to resolve is placement. In print books, pull quotes and sidebars are often placed wherever they fit within the layout, such as on a page that does not have any other special formatting or images. These elements may not make sense in the text where they would be automatically placed by the conversion process, so you should ensure that they are moved in front of the paragraph to which they apply or to another logical place.

Pull Quotes

Formatting pull quotes is actually quite easy. You can place them in `<blockquote>` tags, along with `<hr/>` tags in `<blockquote>` tags above and below, to set them apart from the text.

```
<blockquote><hr/></blockquote>
<blockquote>We must have a concrete idea
of anything, even if it be an imaginary
idea, before we can comprehend
it.</blockquote>
<blockquote><hr/></blockquote>
```

> We must have a concrete idea of anything,
> even if it be an imaginary idea, before we
> can comprehend it.

You could also add a `class="right"` (with the proper CSS) or `align="right"` to the quote's `<blockquote>` tag to give it a right-aligned style.

> We must have a concrete idea of anything,
> even if it be an imaginary idea, before we
> can comprehend it.

As was mentioned above, the Kindle 2 supports the use of HTML tables, but the Kindle 1 does not. The great thing about table support on the Kindle 2 is that tables can have borders and table cells can have a background color. While using tables for tabular data is not suggested, here is a great little hack that lets you format your pull quotes in a way that looks great on the Kindle 2 and still looks good on the Kindle 1.

```
<div align="center">
<table cellpadding="10" style="margin-
left:0;">
    <tr><td><hr width="500" /></td></tr>
    <tr><td align="center" border="1"
    style="background-color:#C0C0C0">We
    must have a concrete idea of anything,
    even if it be an imaginary idea,
    before we can comprehend it.</td></tr>
    <tr><td><hr width="500" /></td></tr>
</table>
</div>
```

The div tag around this pull quote ensures that the table and text are centered on the page. The table contains `cellpadding` attribute with a value of 10 that ensures the table cells have some spacing, and a `margin-left: 0` CSS value that removes the default left margin from the table. The `<hr/>` tags are given a full with, and the middle cell with the text in it has a center alignment, a border, and a background color.

Here is what the above code looks like on the Kindle 2:

And here is what it looks like on the Kindle 1:

The extra spacing below the first `<hr />` tag on the Kindle 1 and the lack of cell padding on the right of the Kindle 2 text are the only issues. Other than that, the pull quote looks good on both devices.

Should you use this hack? That's up to you. The key is to know that there are hacks out there; all you have to do is play with the code.

Sidebars

Sidebars can be formatted in a manner similar to pull quotes. Placing `<hr/>` tags above and below usually works well in showing that the sidebar content is not the main book content, and you could even double the tags to make sure the reader sees them. However, since the text in a sidebar is usually much longer than in a pull quote, formatting the text in `<blockquote>` tags is not usually a good idea. It just makes the text harder to read and makes it fill up more space in the book. You could format it in italics or small caps to make it stand out more, or you might find another format that makes sense in the context of the book design.

However you decide to format them, it is important to make sure the reader can tell the difference between these elements and the regular book text. Without the ability to use background colors, you are limited to using horizontal rules, spacing, and even font size changes in creative ways to accomplish this goal.

Footnotes and Endnotes

A footnote is a note placed at the bottom of the page, while an endnote is a note placed at the end of the chapter or at the end of the book. In Kindle eBooks all footnotes should be converted into endnotes. Since the concept of "pages" is gone, it is much easier to direct the reader to a linked endnote than it is to force them to scroll down and read a footnote that is interjected into the book content. (Note: In this book, I use the term "footnotes" in the more general sense that includes both of these types of notes.)

Linking to a footnote requires the same type of bookmark links you use in the Table of Contents. Within the text, the footnote reference is usually superscripted, and the `<a href="#">` tag can go inside or outside the `<sup>` tags. In the Footnotes section the note number is usually also superscripted, but the `<a name=""/>` should be placed outside the paragraph.

```
<a name="noteref1"/><p>The year 1866 was
signalized<a
href="#note1"><sup>1</sup></a> by a
remarkable incident...</p>
..........
<a name="note1"/><p class="noind"
height="30"><sup>1</sup> To make
conspicuous: distinguish, mark <a
href="#noteref1"><small>[back]</small></a>
</p>
```

On the Kindle 1, when a reader clicks on the line in the text with the superscripted "1" they will be given the option in a pop-up menu to follow the link. On the Kindle 2 the user can navigate the cursor to the link with the joystick and click on it directly. In either case, they will be taken to the correct footnote in your Footnotes section via the anchor tag.

To get back to the text, the user just has to press the Back button on their Kindle. While there is some confusion in the Kindle user community about the functionality of the Back button, most users intuitively understand that they should use it to get back to where they were reading after clicking on a link.

To eliminate confusion and to ensure easy navigation, it is a best practice to also include a link at the end of the footnote back to the beginning of the paragraph where the footnote number is in the book. This also allows the user to peruse the footnotes section independently.

Indexes

An index is an important part of most non-fiction books, and can be valuable for quickly finding specific information or for researching related topics in the book. In Kindle books, the page numbers in indexes can be turned into links to the book text, allowing the user to easily navigate to the content they are researching.

This functionality also utilizes bookmark links, just like the Table of Contents and Footnotes. Your first task is to add a named anchor for each page of the hardcopy into your eBook. Usually the page numbers are ignored in the conversion process from PDF or Microsoft Word into HTML and are not included in the eBook. You will have to go back through the book and add page number anchor tags (e.g., `<a name="page123"/>`) manually to the text of the book. These tags should be added where the top of the page content begins, not the bottom. If a heading or a new paragraph begins at the top of the page, place the anchor outside the heading or paragraph tag.

```
<a name="page123"/><p>My friend the
reporter left me, and I wandered further
afield....</p>
```

If the page begins in the middle of the paragraph, place the anchor in front of the word at the top of the page.

```
<p>Now, I have a mental picture <a
name="page123"/>of John Doe that is as
clear as a steel engraving...</p>
```

If the word is hyphenated across the page break, I usually do not split the word with the anchor tag since that can mess up the search results for that word on the Kindle. Instead, place the anchor after the word and remove the hyphen.

After your page numbers are all added back into the text you can tackle the index formatting. Usually, an index will have two or three levels of indentation underneath main topics. These indentations are most easily formatted with the poetry-type formatting described on page 57. Not only does that formatting allow you to manually adjust the left indent to your liking, it also comes with a built-in hanging indent, making the text much more readable. Your index should look something like this when you are finished:

```
<h3 height="30">D</h3>
<p width="-30">date formats, 24</p>
<p width="-
60">     <i>See
also specific types of transfers</i></p>
<p width="-30">data packets</p>
<p width="-
60">     bus
protocol overview, 22</p>
```

```
<p width="-
60">     packet
field formats, 97-99</p>
<p width="-
60">     in
transfers, 56, 67 <i>Fig. 3</i></p>
<p width="-30">data signal rise and fall
time. <i>See</i> rise and fall times</p>
<h3 height="30">E</h3>
<p width="-30">&ldquo;end&rdquo; encoding,
45</p>
```

When the text is formatted, you can add links to the page numbers. This is most easily done with a regular expression like this:

Find: `(, )([0-9-]+)(-*[0-9]*)`

Replace: `\1<a href="#page\2">\2\3</a>`

That RegEx will find all of the numbers in the index that are preceded by a comma, including page number ranges. With the number links added, you should have something like this:

```
<h3 height="30">D</h3>
<p width="-30">date formats, <a
href="#page24">24</a></p>
<p width="-
60">     <i>See
also specific types of transfers</i></p>
<p width="-30">data packets</p>
<p width="-
60">     bus
protocol overview, <a
href="#page22">22</a></p>
<p width="-
60">     packet
field formats, <a href="#page97">97-
99</a></p>
<p width="-
60">     in
transfers, <a href="#page56">56</a>, <a
```

```
href="#page67fig3">67 <i>Fig.
3</i></a></p>
<p width="-30">data signal rise and fall
time. <i>See</i> <a
href="#riseandfalltimes">rise and fall
times</a></p>
<h3 height="30">E</h3>
<p width="-30">&ldquo;end&rdquo; encoding,
<a href="#page45">45</a></p>
```

D

date formats, 24

See also specific types of transfers

data packets

bus protocol overview, 22

packet field formats, 97-99

in transfers, 56, 67 Fig. 3

data signal rise and fall time. See rise and fall

times

E

"end" encoding, 45

Notice that the page range is only linked to the beginning page. The reader can easily move forward in the book from that point, so there is no need to split the numbers out and link each one. Also, the link to Figure 3 on page 67 is not a regular page number link. I do suggest that you take the reader directly to the item they are being pointed to, especially when that item is not the first thing on the page. In addition, the "See" link is pointing the reader to another section of the Index. The link name can be anything you want, but I suggest leaving it similar to the topic text, but without any spaces. You will need to add an `<a name=""/>` tag in front of that entry in the index.

On the Kindle 1, when the user clicks their scroll-wheel on the line of their choice, a dropdown menu will appear with a list of the active links on that line. If any of your index items has a long list of numbers, you will need to add some `<br/>` tags to the paragraph to break it up a bit. The drop-down menu only shows a total of 13 items, and then only when none of those items is long enough to wrap in the menu.

If your index is long, you will probably want to add a list of alphabetical links at the top of the index so that your users can easily skip around and find what they are looking for. For example:

```
<p class="center"><a
href="#indexA">A</a>   |  &nb
sp;<a
href="#indexB">B</a>   |  &nb
sp;<a
href="#indexC">C</a>   |  &nb
sp;<a
href="#indexD">D</a>   |  &nb
sp;<a href="#indexE">E</a><br />
<a
href="#indexF">F</a>   |  &nb
sp;<a
href="#indexG">G</a>   |  &nb
sp;<a
href="#indexH">H</a>   |  &nb
sp;<a
href="#indexI">I</a>   |  &nb
sp;<a href="#indexJ">J</a><br />
<a
href="#indexK">K</a>   |  &nb
sp;<a
href="#indexL">L</a>   |  &nb
sp;<a
href="#indexM">M</a>   |  &nb
sp;<a
href="#indexN">N</a>   |  &nb
sp;<a href="#indexO">O</a><br />
```

```
<a
href="#indexP">P</a>   | &nb
sp;<a
href="#indexQ">Q</a>   | &nb
sp;<a
href="#indexR">R</a>   | &nb
sp;<a
href="#indexS">S</a>   | &nb
sp;<a href="#indexT">T</a><br />
<a
href="#indexU">U</a>   | &nb
sp;<a
href="#indexV">V</a>   | &nb
sp;<a
href="#indexW">W</a>   | &nb
sp;<a
href="#indexX">X</a>   | &nb
sp;<a
href="#indexY">Y</a>   | &nb
sp;<a href="#indexZ">Z</a></p>
```

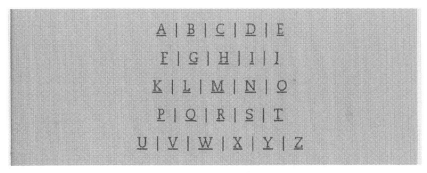

Notice that I have used four non-breaking spaces and a vertical line (|) to separate the letters. Those could be replaced with only non-breaking spaces, with commas, or with anything else that breaks up the letters a little. Also, I centered the list using the stylesheet class name "center" discussed on page 55.

The subheadings for your index will need anchors to match these links, and you may want to add a page break in front of each subheading to break up the list.

Chapter 7

Creating a Mobipocket eBook

Amazon's purchase of Mobipocket in 2005 gave them a soild foundational format on which to base their Kindle books. While the ePub format offers more formatting options and supports more CSS rules, the Mobipocket format is certainly robust enough to handle a large array of book types.

Since the Kindle format is essentially the Mobipocket format, the DTP will automatically create a basic Mobipocket book from the files you upload. If you give it a Word document, you will get the same essential results from the DTP that you would get from loading that Word document into the Mobipocket Creator software. If you upload your source HTML, the process works the same way.

However, there are some tangible benefits to creating your own Mobipocket file and uploading that to the DTP. (Also, if you are large publisher who is providing books to Amazon directly, you are much better off handling this part of the process yourself if at all possible.)

One main benefit is the addition of a key navigation feature to the final book on the Kindle 2. If you add a `toc.ncx` file to your Mobipocket book as described below, the Kindle 2 will include navigational waypoints along the path of your book. A Kindle 2 user could then click the joystick right or left when reading to move between these waypoints. Unfortunately, this feature is not available on the Kindle 1.

Another benefit to making a Mobipocket file is that it gives you the opportunity to sell your book through Mobipocket's eBookBase, an eBook distribution system that reaches many more readers through a long list of online retailers. In addition, there are other marketing and sales opportunities that become available when you have your file in the widely-accepted Mobipocket format.

A third potential benefit of creating a Mobipocket file is the ability to encrypt your Kindle book with Digital Rights Management (DRM), if you are so inclined. Books uploaded to the DTP as an HTML file will be sold in a DRM-free format. That means the purchaser can change the extension on the AZW file to PRC and read the book on any Mobipocket-supported device or on a PC. DRM locks the AZW file specifically to the purchaser's Kindle account. If you want your book to be sold with DRM encryption, you can create a DRMed Mobipocket file and upload that to Amazon. Without getting into the pros and cons of using DRM here, I will say that I usually suggest to my clients that they not use DRM, since it removes the ability for the purchaser of the book to transfer it between devices, effectively tying the user to one device for as long as they own the book.

Getting Set Up

Now that you know the reasons why to create a Mobipocket file, let's talk about how to get ready to do that. First, Mobipocket Creator, the program you will be using, only runs on Windows. If you are using a Mac or Linux computer you will need to switch over to a Windows machine to use the software. There are some other programs that will create a Mobipocket file from a variety of file types (the best I knoiw of is calibre — http://calibre.kovidgoyal.net/), but think Mobipocket Creator is the easiest to use, especially since it is made for that one purpose. You can download Mobipocket Creator here:

http://www.mobipocket.com/en/downloadSoft/ProductDetailsCreator.asp

Once you have installed it, open the program and you will be taken to the Home screen. The Home screen gives you a variety of options for creating new Mobipocket books, importing and converting a book, and publishing books to Mobipocket's eBookBase. When you create or import a file in Mobipocket, the program will save your file to a default Publications location, usually in your Documents directory. If you would like to change that default directory, you can do so using the Settings button at the top of the window.

Importing and Preparing the Book

To import your HTML file into Creator, drag and drop it onto the Creator Window. Alternatively, you can click on "Import from Existing File, HTML Document", then click the Browse button and find the HTML file that way. If you want to make the Publications directory for this book different than the default, you can make that change on the Import page. When you are ready, Click the Import button and click Save at the top of the Creator window.

Go to the Publication directory and open the folder for your book. Inside you will see a copy of the HTML file you imported, as well as an OPF file. The Open Packaging Format (OPF) is a standard XML format for ePub and Mobipocket eBooks that ties together the various pieces of the text. The data you input into Creator will be saved in this OPF file, but you can also easily edit or create the file in a text editor like Notepad++.

Here is a sample OPF file:

```
<?xml version="1.0" encoding="utf-8"?>
<package unique-identifier="uid">
  <metadata>
    <dc-metadata
    xmlns:dc="http://purl.org/metadata/dublin
    _core"
    xmlns:oebpackage="http://openebook.org/na
    mespaces/oeb-package/1.0/">
      <dc:Title>The Four Million</dc:Title>
      <dc:Language>en-us</dc:Language>
      <dc:Identifier
      id="uid">2402C08241</dc:Identifier>
      <dc:Creator>Henry, O.</dc:Creator>
```

```
      <dc:Publisher>eBook
      Architects</dc:Publisher>
      <dc:Subject
      BASICCode="FIC000000">General
      Fiction</dc:Subject>
      <dc:Description>25 delightful tales by
      O. Henry, the master of the surprise
      ending.</dc:Description>
      <dc:Date>03/19/2009</dc:Date>
    </dc-metadata>
    <x-metadata>
      <output encoding="utf-8" content-
      type="text/x-oeb1-document"></output>
      <EmbeddedCover>cover.jpg</EmbeddedCover
      >
      <SRP Currency="USD">0.99</SRP>
      <Demo>FourMillionSample.prc</Demo>
    </x-metadata>
  </metadata>
  <manifest>
    <item id="item1" media-type="text/x-oeb1-
    document" href="FourMillion.html"></item>
    <item id="toc" media-type="application/x-
    dtbncx+xml" href="toc.ncx"></item>
  </manifest>
  <spine toc="toc">
    <itemref idref="item1"/>
  </spine>
  <tours></tours>
  <guide>
    <reference type="toc" title="Table of
    Contents"
    href="FourMillion.html%23TOC"></reference
    >
    <reference type="start" title="Startup
    Page"
    href="FourMillion.html%23start"></referen
    ce>
  </guide>
</package>
```

As you can see, the data in the file is pretty straightforward. It has metadata about the book, a manifest of the files associated with it, and a guide that helps with navigation. These pieces are almost all added within the Mobipocket interface, so there will be very little you need to do within this XML code.

You will also need to copy any image files you have to this Publication directory.

Cover Image

Now that your file is imported, you can start adding the metadata and preparing to build your book. On the left side of the Creator window you will see a list of options. Select Cover Image from this list.

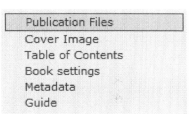

The cover image you insert into Creator needs to be at least 1200 pixels on the long side. Larger is fine, but 1200px seems to work well and does not increase the eBook file size too much. You can leave the cover image in color and at its default DPI.

This brings up another benefit to creating a Mobipocket file for your book: when the book is loaded onto the Kindle 2, the cover image will default to display full-screen, without any of the header or footer information, which makes it look very nice on the Kindle 2 screen.

Make sure you press the Update button below the cover image when you are finished selecting the right one.

Table of Contents

The next item in the options menu is the Table of Contents. If you did not create a TOC earlier in your process, you can use the automated system here to generate a TOC file based on your book's headings. I do not suggest using this feature because you have more control over the formatting when you create it yourself.

However, there is another very important feature concerning the Table of Contents that should not be ignored. As I mentioned at the beginning of this chapter, there is a toc.ncx file that allows users of the Kindle 2 to easily navigate within a book, using the joystick to jump between chapters. This NCX file follows another XML format that is part of the ePub standard. Here is a sample NCX file:

```
<?xml version="1.0" encoding="UTF-8"?>
<!DOCTYPE ncx PUBLIC "-//NISO//DTD ncx 2005-
1//EN" "http://www.daisy.org/z3986/2005/ncx-
2005-1.dtd">
<ncx xmlns="http://www.daisy.org/
z3986/2005/ncx/" version="2005-1">
<docTitle>
  <text>The Four Million</text>
</docTitle>
<navMap>
  <navPoint id="navPoint-1" playOrder="1">
    <navLabel>
      <text>Chapter 1</text>
    </navLabel>
    <content src="book.html#start"/>
    <navPoint id="navPoint-2" playOrder="2">
      <navLabel>
        <text>Subheading 1</text>
      </navLabel>
      <content src="book.html#sub1"/>
    </navPoint>
    <navPoint id="navPoint-3" playOrder="3">
      <navLabel>
        <text>Subheading 2</text>
      </navLabel>
      <content src="book.html#sub2"/>
    </navPoint>
  </navPoint>
  <navPoint id="navPoint-4" playOrder="4">
    <navLabel>
      <text>Chapter 2</text>
    </navLabel>
    <content src="book.html#chap2"/>
  </navPoint>
```

```
    </navMap>
    </ncx>
```

As you can see, the NCX file has essentially the same information as your TOC. The TOC info is broken down into a nested structure, with each element enclosed in a `navPoint` tag. That tag is given a unique `id` and `playOrder`, both of which can be sequential numbers. You can choose to include only your top-level headings, or you can include more headings. The text of the heading is placed inside a `navLabel` tag, and the source of that heading is included in the `content` tag.

Once the NCX file is created, you will need to make sure it is mentioned in the manifest and spine in your OPF file, as was shown in the sample OPF above:

```
<manifest>
  <item id="item1" media-type="text/x-oeb1-
  document" href="FourMillion.html"></item>
  <item id="toc" media-type="application/x-
  dtbncx+xml" href="toc.ncx"></item>
</manifest>
<spine toc="toc">
  <itemref idref="item1"/>
</spine>
```

The item is given a specific media type of `application/x-dtbncx+xml` and the spine is linked to the item's `id`.

Book Settings

The next item in the options list is the Book Settings. If your book includes any Unicode text (see page 93), you should set the Encoding to UTF-8. Also, go ahead and set the book type to eBook. Be sure to press Update when you are done making changes.

Metadata

The metadata section gathers basic information about your book and its contents. For publishing on the Kindle, this same information will need to be inserted into the DTP. For publishing on Mobipocket, the information will be inserted into the eBookBase.

Be sure that the Author name(s) are inserted as "last, first" and separate multiples with semicolons. Select an appropriate subject, fill in the description, and give the file a suggested retail price. You will see the cover image already included if you added one in the Cover Image section earlier. The other sections are optional and can be filled in if you like.

Be sure to press the Update button when you are done.

Guide

The Guide allows the TOC and start anchors you placed in your HTML to be turned into selectable links in the book menu on the Kindle or in Mobipocket Reader. In addition, there are other default Guide items to choose from such as Preface, Foreword, Copyright, and Glossary. Those will not show up in the Kindle menu, but they will show up in Mobipocket. You can also specify your own guide items.

The Filename link can either point to a distinct file name or to an anchor, like this: "`FourMillion.html#start`".

Be sure to press the Update button when you are done.

If you leave out this step, be aware that the book menu in the Kindle will not contain active links to the Table of Contents and the Beginning of the book that you marked with the `<a name="TOC"/>` and `<a name="start"/>` tags. It is important to create the Guide every time you make a Mobipocket file.

Building the Book

When you have finished filling out the details of your book, be sure to push the Save button again. Then, you are ready to build the book.

On the Build page, leave the compression set to Standard, and, at least at first, leave the Encryption Options set to No Encryption. Press the Build button. If there are errors, look at the Build Details and read the error messages. The most common messages are related to the cover image being missing or too small, or to links within your HTML not working. This is actually a great way to test the links in your book after you add a linked index (page 114), footnotes (page 113), or a Table of Contents (page 104). Make sure that any changes you make to the HTML file are done in both the master HTML in your book folder and in the HTML in your Publications folder. I usually just move the OPF file to my main book folder and open it from there so that there is no confusion.

Conclusion

Once your book has successfully been built, you are ready to move on to the previewing and publishing phase. The next chapter will cover those parts of the process.

The source code for the O. Henry book I used in this explanation, including the toc.ncx file and the OPF file, is available in the book downloads section on my website.

This process can be automated for large book jobs using the Mobigen tool available on Mobipocket's website. Mobigen is a command line tool that allows you to do the same building functions as Mobipocket Creator. With the right information and some programming, you could also build the OPF and NCX files on the fly, thus automating the whole Mobipocket creation process.

http://www.mobipocket.com/dev/

Chapter 8

Previewing and Publishing

After your book has been cleaned up and formatted, you will need to take a look at it to make sure that there are no outstanding problems and that the formatting looks the way you want it to look.

Before you pursue either of the preview options below, it would be best to take a quick peek at your HTML file in a Web browser. The formatting will look completely different there than it will look on the Kindle since the default Kindle styles are not applied, but this is an effective way to find heading, block quote, bold, and italics tags that are not closed properly. Just double-click on the HTML file to open it in whatever browser you normally use and scroll through the book looking for issues in those areas. They are usually hard to miss since an unclosed tag will affect the rest of the document. If you make changes to the HTML file, you can go back to the Web browser and refresh the page (usually by pressing F5 on your keyboard), or just close that browser window or tab and open the HTML file again.

Previewing on a Kindle, the Best Way

If you have a Kindle of your own, or have access to one owned by a friend, you should definitely view your book on the actual device. To do that, you will need to get the HTML file into a format that the Kindle accepts. You cannot just copy HTML files directly onto the Kindle; they must either be in the Amazon Kindle's .AZW format or in the Mobipocket format.

Option 1: Load the HTML File on Your Kindle

If your book does not have images, you can e-mail the Kindle-ready HTML file directly to your Kindle, or you can have it e-mailed to you for manual upload. See below (after Option 2) for instructions on both of these methods. You cannot e-mail more than one file to your Kindle at time (not even if they are zipped up together), so if your book has images you will need to use Option 2.

Option 2: Create a Mobipocket Book

Since the Kindle reads unlocked Mobipocket PRC files natively, creating a Mobipocket file is the easiest way to see what your book looks like on the Kindle, especially if the book has images. To create a Mobipocket file, just follow the instructions in Chapter 7. I consider this to be the best approach to testing and publishing a Kindle book, so I highly suggest you use this option.

How to E-mail the Book File to Your Kindle

You can send the Kindle-ready HTML or PRC file directly to your Kindle, or you can have it e-mailed to you for manual upload. To do this, you will need to know the kindle.com address that is assigned to your device. You can find and change this address easily. Just go to the Amazon.com website, log into your account, click on the "Your Account" link at the top of the page, and scroll down to click on the "Manage Your Kindle" link.

At the top of that page you will find a section that allows you to view or change the e-mail account assigned to your Kindle

(for example, myname@kindle.com).

If you send an e-mail to that account with your HTML or PRC file attached, it will be sent to your Kindle over Whispernet. If you would prefer to load the book on your Kindle manually, or are not in an area with Whispernet access, you can send the book to your free.kindle.com address

(for example, myname@free.kindle.com)

and the converted Amazon AZW file will be e-mailed back to you. You must also make sure that the e-mail address from which you are sending the book is listed in your approved e-mail list on the Manage Your Kindle page.

How to Manually Copy the Book File to Your Kindle

To manually upload a book to your Kindle, you must have a USB cable, which ships with the device. If you have lost this cable, you can purchase a replacement at from Amazon.

Plug the large connector into a USB port on your computer, and plug the small connector into the bottom of the Kindle. Your Kindle screen will change to a message about it being plugged in.

Now, go to "My Computer" (or Finder on Mac) and you will see the Kindle listed like a drive in the list. Open the Kindle folder, and you will see some subfolders. The "documents" folder is where all of your book content is stored. If you are uploading a file that Amazon converted via e-mail, or a Mobipocket book you created, just place it in that folder.

Once you are finished copying the file over, close the Kindle folder window. In Windows, eject the Kindle using the "Safely Remove Hardware" icon in your System Tray, and unplug the Kindle when you are told it is safe. On a Mac, eject the Kindle as you would normally eject a disk. Then unplug the USB cable from the bottom of the Kindle.

Once your Kindle is switched back from USB mode, go to your Home screen and find the book you just uploaded.

Previewing on the DTP

The second-best option for previewing your book is to use the Preview tool on the DTP Dashboard. To upload the book, log into the DTP Dashboard at http://dtp.amazon.com/. If you do not have the book set up in the Dashboard yet, click the "Add new item" button. Go to "2. Upload and Preview Book." Click on the Browse button and find the file you would like to upload. If your book has images, you will need to zip up the images and the HTML into one zip file, and upload that to the Dashboard. If you have a PRC file, just upload that alone.

Once the file has been uploaded and converted, you can click on the Preview button to take a look at it. The DTP Preview window is not a perfect emulator of the Kindle device, so there are some pretty important issues you need to keep in mind as you are looking at your book.

1. The Preview is currently still displaying text using the version 1.1.1 engine. This means that the updates that were released for the Kindle 1 with version 1.2 as well as the new functions (like tables) that are available in the Kindle 2 will not be formatted properly on the Preview Screen.

2. The font sizes are not the same as the Kindle font sizes; however, they are close, and there is enough distinction between them to get a good approximation of actual formatting.

3. The images in the Preview are not shown exactly as they would look on the Kindle screen, mostly because you are not viewing the book with an e-Ink screen. The images actually look more like they would look in a screen shot created by the Kindle, and that may very well be what the Preview tool does to show you the book.

4. The Preview shows the bookmark links in your book in blue so that you can see what is linking and what is not linking. They will not be blue on the device.

5. The Preview does not include the header and the author's name, nor does it include the status/menu bar at the bottom of the screen.

Overall, the current Preview screen is much better than the one Amazon originally made available, and it is possible to get a good idea what the book will look like on the Kindle.

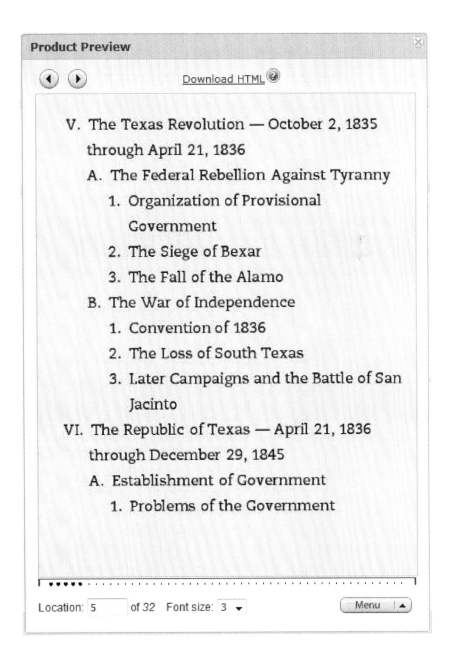

Product Preview

Download HTML

V. The Texas Revolution — October 2, 1835 through April 21, 1836

   A. The Federal Rebellion Against Tyranny

      1. Organization of Provisional Government

      2. The Siege of Bexar

      3. The Fall of the Alamo

   B. The War of Independence

      1. Convention of 1836

      2. The Loss of South Texas

      3. Later Campaigns and the Battle of San Jacinto

VI. The Republic of Texas — April 21, 1836 through December 29, 1845

   A. Establishment of Government

      1. Problems of the Government

Location: 5   of 32 Font size: 3 ▾   Menu ▲

Publishing Your Book

To publish your book on the Amazon DTP, all you need to do is fill in the three sections under the book title (*Enter Product Details*, *Upload & Preview Book*, and *Enter Price*). The sections are fairly self-explanatory. Once you are finished filling out the required information, a Publish button will appear. When you press that button the process will be started to publish your book on the Amazon Kindle store, and you will not be able to make more changes or upload a new file until the process is complete. The book will show up for sale sometime between 12 and 72 hours after that button-press, but the description and cover image may take a little bit longer to show up on the product page.

If you want to sell the book in the Mobipocket format as well, you can choose skip the DTP publication process and only publish the book through Mobipocket. This is because Mobipocket will allow you to distribute your book to the Kindle, as well as to dozens of other eBook sites. Mobipocket and Amazon both pay a 35% royalty for eBook sales. However, Amazon will pay you royalties 60 days after each monthly period as long as you have accrued at least $10, while Mobipocket officially states that it can withhold your royalties until you have accrued $150. Also, be aware that when you publish through Mobipocket you cannot track the individual sales of an eBook on the Amazon Kindle store.

I usually suggest to my clients that they publish on the two stores separately, and just de-select Amazon from the list of approved retailers Mobipocket can distribute to.

The Mobipocket publication process is beyond the scope of this book, but I have created a video tutorial on my website that takes you through the process step-by-step.

A Note about Digital Rights Management (DRM): Books uploaded to the DTP as an HTML file will be sold in a DRM-free format. That means the purchaser can change the extension on the AZW file to PRC and read the book on a Mobipocket-supported device. If you want your book to be sold with DRM encryption, you will need to create a DRMed Mobipocket file and upload that to the DTP.

Conclusion and Formatting Services

Well, that's it! Hopefully by this point you have found answers to all of your questions and have successfully published your book on the Amazon Kindle. If you have hit a brick wall or need help with the process, or if your book is just too difficult for you to format yourself, I stand ready to assist you in any way I can.

I offer a range of services to authors and publishers, including:

- **Full-service eBook preparation and formatting**: I can take your file or hard copy book and turn it into a fully-functional, beautifully formatted Kindle eBook. This full-service option leaves you with no need to delve into the HTML, or worry about the final appearance of your Kindle book. In addition, if you have purchased a copy of this book and have found the process to be more than you want to tackle, I will discount the sale price of this book off the cost of your eBook preparation. Just send me a copy of your receipt.
- **File conversions**: Sometimes all you need is the ability to get your book into HTML. I can convert your PDF or Word document into useable HTML if you are unable to do that conversion yourself.
- **Hard copy conversions**: OCRing a book is not always an easy process, and can become an expensive endeavor if you try to do it all yourself. I use the best OCR software available, and my thorough file

preparation will leave you with a digital file that can be easily reformatted for print or for eBook publishing.

- **Code cleanup**: If you want to do the formatting yourself, but the initial HTML cleanup is making you sweat, I can do the major code cleanup, giving you an HTML file that will be easy for you to format with headings, margins, etc., as explained in this book.
- **Troubleshooting and error-checking**: If you are stumped with a formatting issue and you just need someone to fix the problem, I can do that for you very easily.
- **Screen shots**: Since the DTP Preview does such a bad job of showing what a book looks like on the Kindle, I can take screen shots of key pages in your book on my Kindle, allowing you to see how your formatting process is going.
- **Mobipocket File Creation**: In addition to formatting your book, I can also create the Mobipocket file you can upload to the Mobipocket eBookBase.
- **Publisher Consultations**: As a long-time eBook professional I am well-versed in the preparation and delivery of digital book content. If you are a publisher looking to set up an eBook conversion process in-house or working on any other eBook project, I would be more than happy assist you.
- **Other services**: I am available for other eBook-related services as well. Please drop me a line if you have any questions or need my help in any way. Also, be sure to check out my websites for information about other services that are not listed here.

Joshua Tallent

eBook Architects LLC

http://eBookArchitects.com

http://KindleFormatting.com

joshua@kindleformatting.com

512-939-3466

Appendix A

Supported HTML and CSS

Miscellaneous Tags

`<!--...-->`	Comment. Not displayed in the book. (page 92)
`<a href="">...</a>`	Links to a bookmark anchor ("#bookmarkname") or to an external website. (page 89)
`<a name="">...</a>`	Establishes an internal bookmark to which you can link. (page 89)
`<html>...</html>`	The opening and closing tags in your document.
`<head>...</head>`	Contains information about the HTML document, such as <link>, <title>, and <style> tags.
`<body>...</body>`	Contains the contents of the book.
`<hr />`	Creates a line (horizontal rule). (page 91)
`<img src="" alt="" />`	Inserts an image. (page 74)
`<mbp:pagebreak/>`	Page break. (page 92)

Font Formatting

Font Size

`<small>...</small>`	Reduces font size to one level smaller than the current font size. (page 44)
`<big>...</big>`	Increases font size to one level larger than the current font size. (page 42)

Italics

`<i>...</i>`	Italic. (page 43)
`<em>...</em>`	Emphasized text (italicized). (page 43)
`<cite>...</cite>`	Indicates that enclosed text is quoted from another source (italicized).
`<var>...</var>`	Indicates a variable name or program argument (italicized).

Bold

`<b>...</b>`	Bold (page 43)
`<strong>...</strong>`	Strong emphasis (bold). (page 43)

Lines

`<u>...</u>`	Underlined. (page 44)
`<s>...</s>`	Strikethrough. (page 46)
`<strike>...</strike>`	Strikethrough. (page 46)

Mono-spaced

`<code>...</code>`	Computer code. (page 47)
`<kbd>...</kbd>`	Keyboard text. (page 47)
`<samp>...</samp>`	Sample text. (page 47)
`<tt>...</tt>`	Teletype text. (page 47)

Other

`<span>...</span>`	Generic tag; can be used to apply a variety of styles. (page 47)
`<sub>...</sub>`	Reduces the font size and drops the text below the baseline. (page 45)
`<sup>...</sup>`	Reduces the font size and raises the text to the top of the line. (page 45)

Paragraphs, etc.

`<h1>...</h1>`	Heading tags. (page 67)
`<h2>...</h2>`	
`<h3>...</h3>`	
`<h4>...</h4>`	
`<h5>...</h5>`	
`<h6>...</h6>`	
`<div>...</div>`	Division or section. (page 59)
`<p>...</p>`	Paragraph. (page 48)

`<blockquote>...` `</blockquote>`	Long quote. Creates left margin of 0.5 inches. (page 59)
` `	Line break. (page 58)
`<center>...</center>`	Centers content horizontally. (page 55)
`<ol>...</ol>`	Numbered list. Use `<li>` tags inside. (page 63)
`<ul>...</ul>`	Bulleted list. Use `<li>` tags inside. (page 63)
`<li>...</li>`	List item. (page 63)

Common Attributes in HTML Tags

`class`	Allows you to set a style in the style sheet to be used in multiple tags
`name`	Used in `<a>` tags to assign a bookmark name. (page 89)
`width`	Adjusts the first-line indent of a paragraph, blockquote, heading, and list tags. Negative creates a hanging indent. Supports pixels (`width="30"`), points (`width="10pt"`), percent (`width="10%"`), or *em*-units (`width="3em"`). (page 51)
`height`	Sets a top margin on a paragraph, blockquote, heading, and list tags. Supports pixels (`height="30"`), points (`height="10pt"`), percent (`height="10%"`), or *em*-units (`height="3em"`). (page 68)
`style`	Allows the inclusion of CSS styles in a specific tag.

align	Aligns the text in paragraph, blockquote, heading, and list tags. Supports values of `left`, `right`, and `center`.

Supported CSS

Font

Property	Description	Values
font-size	Sets the size of a font	xx-small
		x-small
		small
		medium
		large
		x-large
		xx-large
		length
		%
font-style	Sets the style of the font	normal
		italic
		oblique
font-weight	Sets the weight of a font	normal
		bold

Positioning

Property	Description	Values
vertical-align	Sets the vertical alignment of an element	sub
		super

Text

Property	Description	Values
text-align	Aligns the text in an element	left
		right
		center
		justify
text-decoration	Adds decoration to text	underline
		line-through
text-indent	Indents the first line of text in an element	*length*
		%

Appendix B

Regular Expressions

Regular Expressions make eBook development take much less time. This list of Regular Expression operators covers what is supported in Notepad++, an easy-to-use open source text editor. If you are using a different editor, be sure to check its Help files for information on Regular Expressions it supports. Not all editors are the same, but there should be similarities in what operators are supported. See page 26 for more information.

.	(period) Matches any character
(. . .)	This marks a region for tagging a match; the contents inside ( ) can be re-inserted in "replace with" using \1, \2 etc.
\n	**Replace Only:** Where n is 1 through 9, referring to the first through ninth tagged region when replacing. For example, if the search string was Fred([1-9])YYY and the replace string was Sam\1ZZZ , when applied to Fred2XXX this would generate Sam2YYY.
\<	This matches the start of a word.
\>	This matches the end of a word.

\x	This allows you to use a character x that would otherwise have a special meaning. For example, \. would be interpreted as an actual period and not "any character."
[...]	This indicates a set of characters, for example, [abc] means any of the characters a, b or c. You can also use ranges, for example [a-z] for any lower case character or [0-9] for any number.
[^...]	Anything except the characters in the set. For example, [^A-Za-z] means any character except an alphabetic character.
^	This matches the start of a line (unless used inside brackets, see above).
$	This matches the end of a line.
*	This matches the preceding item 0 or more times. For example, Sa*m matches Sm, Sam, Saam, Saaam, etc.; [a-z]* matches any number of lowercase letters.
+	This matches the preceding item 1 or more times. For example, Sa+m matches Sam, Saam, Saaam, etc.

Appendix C

HTML Character Entities

Below you will find a list of common Latin-1 characters as well as some of the special symbols that are supported on the Kindle. Each character includes the decimal, hexadecimal and/or named HTML entity that should be used when formatting that character in your eBook. On page 155 there is a master list of the Unicode character sets supported on the Kindle.

`&hellip;`	`&#133;`	…	elipses
`&lsquo;`	`&#145;`	'	open single quote
`&rsquo;`	`&#146;`	'	close single quote
`&ldquo;`	`&#147;`	"	close double quotes
`&rdquo;`	`&#148;`	"	open double quotes
`&bull;`	`&#149;`	•	bullet
`&middot;`	`&#183;`	·	middle dot
`&ndash;`	`&#150;`	–	en dash
`&mdash;`	`&#151;`	—	em dash
`&tilde;`	`&#152;`	~	tilde

&trade;	&#153;	™	trademark
&reg;	&#174;	®	registered trademark
			nonbreaking space
&dagger;	&#134;	†	dagger
&Dagger;	&#135;	‡	double dagger
&iexcl;	&#161;	¡	inverted exclamation
&iquest;	&#191;	¿	inverted question mark
&sect;	&#167;	§	section sign
&para;	&#182;	¶	paragraph sign
&fnof;	&#131;	ƒ	function
&permil;	&#137;	‰	per mill sign
&deg;	&#176;	°	degree sign
&plusmn;	&#177;	±	plus or minus
&times;	&#215;	×	multiplication sign
&divide;	&#247;	÷	division sign
&sup1;	&#185;	^{1}	superscript one
&sup2;	&#178;	^{2}	superscript two
&sup3;	&#179;	^{3}	superscript three
&micro;	&#181;	µ	micro sign
&cent;	&#162;	¢	cent sign
&pound;	&#163;	£	pound sterling

`&yen;`	`&#165;`	¥	yen sign
`&frac14;`	`&#188;`	¼	one-fourth
`&frac12;`	`&#189;`	½	one-half
`&frac34;`	`&#190;`	¾	three-fourths
`&Agrave;`	`&#192;`	À	uppercase A, grave
`&Aacute;`	`&#193;`	Á	uppercase A, acute
`&Acirc;`	`&#194;`	Â	uppercase A, circumflex
`&Atilde;`	`&#195;`	Ã	uppercase A, tilde
`&Auml;`	`&#196;`	Ä	uppercase A, umlaut
`&Aring;`	`&#197;`	Å	uppercase A, ring
`&AElig;`	`&#198;`	Æ	uppercase AE
`&Ccedil;`	`&#199;`	Ç	uppercase C, cedilla
`&Egrave;`	`&#200;`	È	uppercase E, grave
`&Eacute;`	`&#201;`	É	uppercase E, acute
`&Ecirc;`	`&#202;`	Ê	uppercase E, circumflex
`&Euml;`	`&#203;`	Ë	uppercase E, umlaut
`&Igrave;`	`&#204;`	Ì	uppercase I, grave
`&Iacute;`	`&#205;`	Í	uppercase I, acute
`&Icirc;`	`&#206;`	Î	uppercase I, circumflex
`&Iuml;`	`&#207;`	Ï	uppercase I, umlaut
`&ETH;`	`&#208;`	Ð	uppercase Eth, Icelandic

&Ntilde;	&#209;	Ñ	uppercase N, tilde
&Ograve;	&#210;	Ò	uppercase O, grave
&Oacute;	&#211;	Ó	uppercase O, acute
&Ocirc;	&#212;	Ô	uppercase O, circumflex
&Otilde;	&#213;	Õ	uppercase O, tilde
&Ouml;	&#214;	Ö	uppercase O, umlaut
&Oslash;	&#216;	Ø	uppercase O, slash
&OElig;	&#140;	Œ	Capital O-E ligature
&Scaron;	&#138;	Š	Capital S, caron
&Ugrave;	&#217;	Ù	uppercase U, grave
&Uacute;	&#218;	Ú	uppercase U, acute
&Ucirc;	&#219;	Û	uppercase U, circumflex
&Uuml;	&#220;	Ü	uppercase U, umlaut
&Yacute;	&#221;	Ý	uppercase Y, acute
&Yuml;	&#159;	Ÿ	uppercase Y, dieresis
	&#142;	Ž	uppercase Z, hacek
&THORN;	&#222;	Þ	uppercase THORN, Icelandic
&szlig;	&#223;	ß	lowercase sharps, German
&agrave;	&#224;	à	lowercase a, grave
&aacute;	&#225;	á	lowercase a, acute
&acirc;	&#226;	â	lowercase a, circumflex

Appendix C. HTML Character Entities

&atilde;	&#227;	ã	lowercase a, tilde
&auml;	&#228;	ä	lowercase a, umlaut
&aring;	&#229;	å	lowercase a, ring
&aelig;	&#230;	æ	lowercase ae
&ccedil;	&#231;	ç	lowercase c, cedilla
&egrave;	&#232;	è	lowercase e, grave
&eacute;	&#233;	é	lowercase e, acute
&ecirc;	&#234;	ê	lowercase e, circumflex
&euml;	&#235;	ë	lowercase e, umlaut
&igrave;	&#236;	ì	lowercase i, grave
&iacute;	&#237;	í	lowercase i, acute
&icirc;	&#238;	î	lowercase i, circumflex
&iuml;	&#239;	ï	lowercase i, umlaut
&eth;	&#240;	ð	lowercase eth, Icelandic
&ntilde;	&#241;	ñ	lowercase n, tilde
&ograve;	&#242;	ò	lowercase o, grave
&oacute;	&#243;	ó	lowercase o, acute
&ocirc;	&#244;	ô	lowercase o, circumflex
&otilde;	&#245;	õ	lowercase o, tilde
&ouml;	&#246;	ö	lowercase o, umlaut
&oslash;	&#248;	ø	lowercase o, slash

&oelig;	&#156;	œ	oe ligature
&scaron;	&#154;	š	lowercase s, caron
&ugrave;	&#249;	ù	lowercase u, grave
&uacute;	&#250;	ú	lowercase u, acute
&ucirc;	&#251;	û	lowercase u, circumflex
&uuml;	&#252;	ü	lowercase u, umlaut
&yacute;	&#253;	ý	lowercase y, acute
&yuml;	&#255;	ÿ	lowercase y, umlaut
	&#158;	ž	lowercase z, hacek
&thorn;	&#254;	þ	lowercase thorn, Icelandic

Useful Special Symbols

&#x25a0;	&#9632;	■	Big black square
&#x25a1;	&#9633;	□	Big white square
&#x25aa;	&#9642;	▪	Small black square
&#x25ab;	&#9643;	▫	Small white square
&#x25b2;	&#9650;	▲	Big black triangle
&#x25b3;	&#9651;	△	Big white triangle
&#x25b6;	&#9654;	►	Small black arrow right
&#x25b7;	&#9655;	▷	Small white arrow right
&#x25bc;	&#9660;	▼	Big black arrow down

`&#x25bd;`	`&#9661;`	▽	Big white arrow down
`&#x25be;`	`&#9662;`	▼	Small black arrow down
`&#x25bf;`	`&#9663;`	▽	Small white arrow down
`&#x25c2;`	`&#9666;`	◄	Small black arrow left
`&#x25c3;`	`&#9667;`	◁	Small white arrow left
`&#x25ca;`	`&#9674;`	◊	Diamond
`&#x25cb;`	`&#9675;`	○	White circle
`&#x25cf;`	`&#9679;`	●	Black circle
`&#x2190;`	`&#8592;`	←	Left arrow
`&#x2191;`	`&#8593;`	↑	Up arrow
`&#x2192;`	`&#8594;`	→	Right arrow
`&#x2193;`	`&#8595;`	↓	Down arrow
`&#x2194;`	`&#8596;`	↔	Relation
`&#x2245;`	`&#8773;`	≅	Approximately equal to
`&#x2248;`	`&#8776;`	≈	Asymptotic
`&#x2260;`	`&#8800;`	≠	Not equal to
`&#x2261;`	`&#8801;`	≡	Identical to
`&#x2264;`	`&#8804;`	≤	Less than or equal to
`&#x2265;`	`&#8805;`	≥	Greater than or equal to
`&#x2318;`	`&#8984;`	⌘	Command key

&#x23ce;	&#9166;	⏎	Return symbol
&#x2605;	&#9733;	★	Black star
&#x2606;	&#9734;	☆	White star
&#x263a;	&#9786;	☺	White smiling face
&#x263b;	&#9787;	☻	Black smiling face
&#x263c;	&#9788;	☼	White sun with rays
&#x2640;	&#9792;	♀	Female sign
&#x2642;	&#9794;	♂	Male sign
&#x2660;	&#9824;	♠	Spade
&#x2663;	&#9827;	♣	Shamrock
&#x2665;	&#9829;	♥	Heart
&#x2713;	&#10003;	✓	Check mark
&#x2669;	&#9833;	♩	Quarter note
&#x266a;	&#9834;	♪	Eighth note
&#x266b;	&#9835;	♫	Beamed eighth note
&#x266c;	&#9836;	♬	Beamed sixteenth note
&#x266d;	&#9837;	♭	Flat sign
&#x266e;	&#9838;	♮	Natural sign
&#x266f;	&#9839;	♯	Sharp sign

Supported Character Sets

Below are the Unicode character sets supported on the Kindle. For more information about these character sets and what they include, go to http://www.unicode.org/charts/.

Basic Latin (U+0020 - U+007F)

Latin-1 Supplement (U400A0 - U+00FF)

Latin Extended-A (U+0100 - U+017F)

Latin Extended-B (U+0180 - U+Q24f)

IPA Extensions (U+2050 - U+20AF)

Spacing Modifier Letters (U+02B0 - U+02FP)

Greek and Coptic (U+0370 - U+03FF)

Latin Extended - Additional (U+1E00 - U+1EFF)

Greek Extended (U+lF00 - U+IFFF)

General Punctuation (U+2000 - U+206F)

Superscripts and Subscripts (U+2070 - U+209F)

Currency Symbols (U+20A0 - U+20CF)

Letterlike Symbols (U+2100 - U+214F)

Number Forms (U+2150 - U+218F)

Arrows (U+2190 - U+21FF)

Mathematical Operators (U+2200 - U+22FF)

Miscellaneous Technical (U+2300 - U+23FF)

Enclosed Alphanumerics (U+2460 - U+24FF)

Geometric Shapes (U+25A0 - U+25FF)

Miscellaneous Symbols (U+2600 - U+26FF)

Dingbats (U+2700 - U+27BF)

Private Use (U+E000 - U+F8FF)

Alphabetic Presentation Forms (U+FB00 - U+FB4F)

Appendix D

Links and Contacts

This is a compilation of contact information for Amazon, links to informative websites, and helpful tools for your Kindle formatting experience.

Amazon Contacts and Links

DTP technical support:

dtp-feedback@amazon.com

The Digital Publishing Department:

digitalpublications@amazon.com

The Digital Rights Group:

digitalrights@amazon.com

> Contact them if you want to make your book available as a free download on the Amazon Store.

The Digital Text Platform (DTP):

http://dtp.amazon.com

> This is the publishing system for Amazon books.

DTP Forums:

http://forums.digitaltextplatform.com/dtpforums

> These are the official discussion forums for the DTP and Kindle publishing.

Other Websites, Blogs, and Forums

Microsoft Word help:

http://www.shaunakelly.com/word/stylesms

http://editorium.com/

Automated Proofreading with ErrNET:

http://www.errnet.net/

I have a contract with ErrNET. If you want to use their service at a discount, drop me a line.

Mobipocket Creator Download:

http://www.mobipocket.com/dev/

Mobipocket Creator Instructions:

http://www.mobipocket.com/dev/article.asp?BaseFolder=creatorpublisher

Notepad++:

http://notepadplus.sourceforge.net

Kindle-specific Websites:

http://www.kindleboards.com/

http://ireaderreview.com/

http://kindlereader.blogspot.com/

http://kindlehomepage.blogspot.com/

http://www.blogkindle.com/

eBook and Independent Author Websites:

http://www.teleread.org/

http://publetariat.com/

http://www.aprillhamilton.com/iaguides.html

Differences between Kindle 1 and Kindle 2:

http://kindleformatting.com/blog/2009/02/kindle-2-review-formatting-perspective.php

Made in the USA